Vasco Nuñez

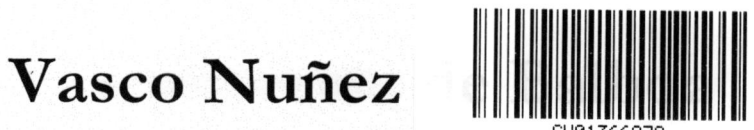

Frederick A. Ober

Alpha Editions

This edition published in 2024

ISBN : 9789362927064

Design and Setting By
Alpha Editions
www.alphaedis.com
Email - info@alphaedis.com

As per information held with us this book is in Public Domain.
This book is a reproduction of an important historical work. Alpha Editions uses the best technology to reproduce historical work in the same manner it was first published to preserve its original nature. Any marks or number seen are left intentionally to preserve its true form.

Contents

I THE MAN-OF-THE-BARREL 1475-1510 .... - 2 -
II LEADER OF A FORLORN HOPE 1510 .... - 10 -
III BALBOA ASSERTS HIS SUPREMACY 1510 .... - 16 -
IV BALBOA CAPTURES A PRINCESS 1511 .... - 22 -
V THE CACIQUES OF DARIEN 1511 .... - 30 -
VI FIRST TIDINGS OF THE PACIFIC 1512 .... - 38 -
VII A SEARCH FOR THE GOLDEN TEMPLE 1511 .... - 44 -
VIII CONSPIRACY OF THE CACIQUES 1512 .... - 48 -
IX HOW THE CONSPIRACY WAS DEFEATED 1512 .... - 54 -
X DISSENSIONS IN THE COLONY 1512 .... - 60 -
XI BALBOA STRENGTHENS HIS ARM 1512 .... - 66 -
XII THE QUEST FOR THE AUSTRAL OCEAN 1513 .... - 72 -
XIII ON THE SHORES OF THE PACIFIC 1513 .... - 79 -
XIV A RIVAL IN THE FIELD 1514 .... - 86 -
XV PEDRARIAS, THE SCOURGE OF DARIEN 1515 .... - 92 -
XVI IN THE DOMAIN OF THE DRAGONS 1515 .... - 98 -
XVII A COMPACT WITH THE ENEMY 1516 .... - 104 -
XVIII BUILDING THE BRIGANTINES 1516 .... - 109 -
XIX IMPRISONED AND IN CHAINS 1517 .... - 115 -
XX THE END OF VASCO NUÑEZ DE BALBOA 1517 ... - 120 -
FOOTNOTES: .... - 125 -

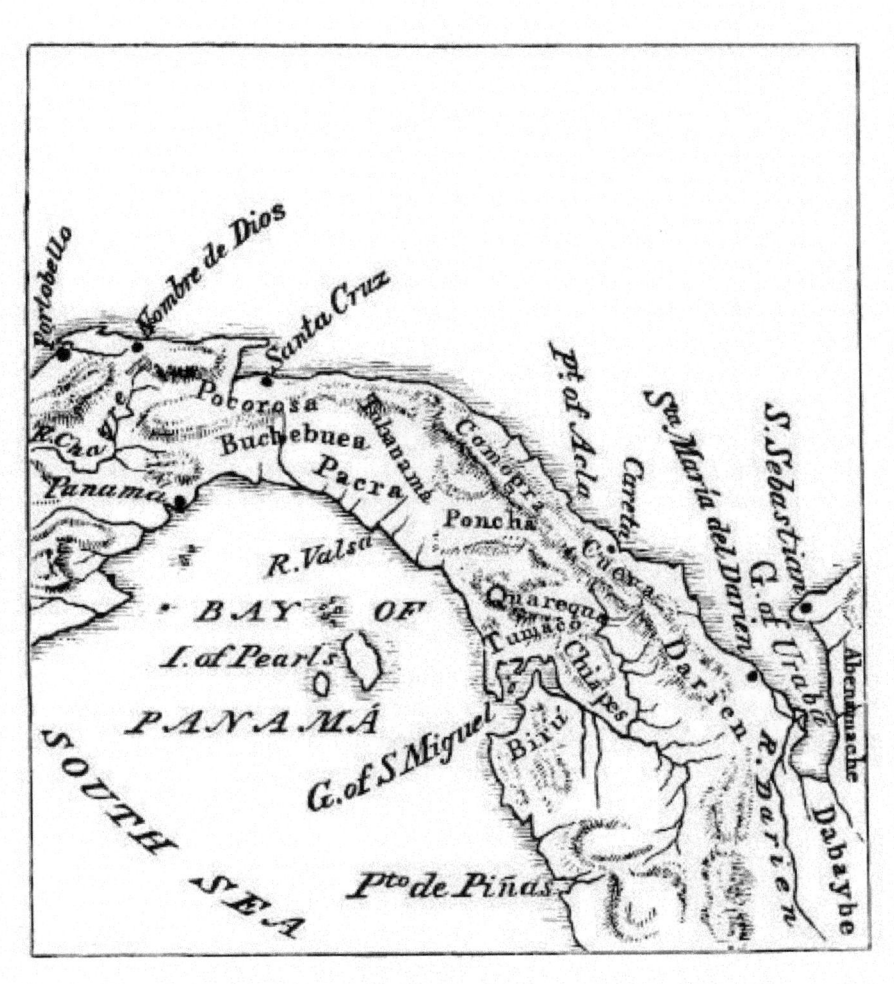

PANAMA, DARIEN, AND THE SOUTH SEA

I

THE MAN-OF-THE-BARREL

1475-1510

SOMETIME in the summer of the year 1501 there landed on the southern coast of Santo Domingo one of the strangest expeditions that ever visited its shores. It was commanded by one Rodrigo de Bastidas, a rich notary of Seville, in Old Spain, who had become imbued with a passion for adventure, and so set forth, with a company contained in two caravels, over the route followed by Christopher Columbus in his third voyage to America. As he was guided by the skilled pilot Juan de la Cosa, who had been with Columbus in the West Indies, his voyage was in every respect successful, save in its ending. It included the entire length of *Terra Firma* (as the north coast of South America was then called), from the Gulf of Maracaibo to the Isthmus of Darien, whence, after profitable bartering with the Indians, Bastidas set sail for Spain.

He had sought traffic only, and not conquest, hence had been everywhere received with open arms by the natives, who poured out their treasures of gold and pearls most lavishly, so that he and all his comrades were enriched. Only one other venture to this region, that of Pedro Niño, the year previous, had yielded such rich returns, and it was with exultation that the members of this expedition turned the prows of their caravels homeward. When half-way across the Caribbean Sea, however, they discovered, to their great alarm, that their vessels were leaking in every part, and upon investigation found the hulls full of holes, made by the destructive teredo, or ship-worm, the existence of which they had not suspected. The nearest land was the island of Santo Domingo, then known as Hispaniola, and, bearing up for it, they found a harbor in the Bay of Ocoa. The caravels were hardly kept afloat until this haven was reached, and foundered in port before their cargoes were landed. All the arms and ammunition aboard, as well as much of the provisions, went down with the vessels; but no lives were lost, and the most precious portion of the cargoes was saved, to the last pearl and nugget of gold.

The governor of Santo Domingo at that time was Don Francisco de Bobadilla, who, though but a year or so in office, had already committed irreparable wrongs upon the natives of the island. But a few months had elapsed since he had sent Christopher Columbus and his brothers home to Spain in chains. Having sequestrated their effects, he was rapidly squandering his ill-gotten wealth, and actually living in the old admiral's castle.

One hot midsummer day, as Governor Bobadilla was enjoying his siesta, or noonday nap, he was rudely awakened by one of his mounted scouts, who had ridden all night and all morning, coming in from the westward. Pushing aside the sentinel on duty in the lower court, he sprang up the stone stairs with jangling spurs, and, making his way to the balcony overlooking the river Ozama, where the governor's hammock was swung, he exclaimed: "Your excellency, I have dire news to report. It calls for immediate action, too, hence my intrusion upon your privacy."

"Ha! it must be pressing, indeed," replied the governor, testily, rubbing his eyes and at the same time rolling out of his hammock. "Know you not, sirrah, that I could have you swung from the battlements—yea, dashed to the pavement of the court below? Ho, it is Enrique! Pardon me, man, I thought it must be some varlet of the admiral's scurvy gang. No chances lose the *Colombinos* [partisans of Columbus] to invade my castle and seek to press home their claims, perchance their rusty blades! But proceed. What is it, Enrique?"

"Your excellency, three bands of lawless adventurers, under one Bastidas and the pilot Juan de la Cosa, are marching through the country, with intent, most probably, of attacking the capital. Each band is provided with a coffer filled with gold and pearls, which they are bestowing upon the Indians in exchange for provisions. They are committing no ravage, being in the main unarmed; but I thought your excellency should be informed, and so have come, as you see, all the way from Azua, without rest."

"As a faithful retainer, Enrique, you have done well, and shall receive your reward. They can do no harm, doubtless, since we are here in force; but, laden with gold and pearls, say you?"

"Yes, your excellency, rioting in wealth, which they have obtained in Terra Firma. Not a man among them that has not great store."

"Ha! They come most opportunely, then, for this island of Hispaniola is wellnigh drained of its riches, what with the ravages of Roldan's men and the license permitted by Bartolomé Colon. Their wealth is, without doubt, ill-gotten, and we must see what can be done with it. Trading without permission, whether on Terra Firma or in the isles, is a serious offence."

"But, excellency, the commander of the expedition is Rodrigo Bastidas, a lawyer of note in Seville, and he claims to have had permission from the sovereigns. He comes not with intent to trade in this island, so he says, but, his vessels having foundered, he desires only assistance to proceed home to Spain."

"And he shall get it, forsooth; but not of the sort he may crave. A lawyer, say you? Well, since I have already incarcerated an admiral, an adelantado, and the governor of this very city of Santo Domingo, it seems not reasonable that I shall be bearded by a bachelor! The dungeon awaits him, and there is a place in my treasury for his store of gold and pearls, until it shall be shown that the royal fifth is secure. Go now and call the captain of the guard. Tell it not in the town; but I shall have my soldiers ready to arrest these marauders the moment they arrive."

The avaricious Bobadilla kept his word to the letter, for when, the next night, his shipwrecked countrymen arrived within sight of the city, they were met by an armed force and conducted, weak and famishing as they were, to the prison-pen, where they were herded like cattle. The rank and file were soon released, and allowed to wander at will about the island, but Bastidas and La Cosa were kept immured for many months. In June or July of the next year they were placed on board one of the ships comprising the large fleet collected by the governor to accompany him to Spain. Bobadilla embarked in another vessel, at the same time, but lost his life in a hurricane, which sank nearly every ship in his fleet.[1]

The vessel containing Bastidas and La Cosa survived the tempest, and they safely arrived in Spain with the greater portion of their treasure. Both received high honors at the hands of their sovereign, and returned to the scenes of their discoveries, on the coast of Terra Firma, where the gallant pilot was killed by a poisoned arrow. Bastidas was appointed governor of Santa Marta, where, because he treated the Indians justly and took their part against his ferocious followers, he was assassinated by some of his own men. His remains were taken to Santo Domingo, and in its cathedral is a chapel dedicated to the memory of "the Adelantado Rodrigo de Bastidas," who, together with his wife and child, there sleeps his last, in a tomb elaborately carved, as attested by an inscription on the chapel wall.

While the adventures of the humane Bastidas were sufficiently interesting to attract attention at the time of their occurrence, they might, possibly, have escaped the historian were it not for the fact that they were shared by a man whose subsequent fortunes were identified with one of the greatest events in American history. This man was Vasco Nuñez de Balboa, who enlisted under Bastidas at Seville, and accompanied him throughout the voyage, with its consequent disasters. He was then an obscure individual, known only as a dependant of Don Pedro Puertocarrero, the mighty lord of Moguer. He was not a native of Moguer (that town near Palos so closely identified with Columbus and the discovery of America), but came from Xeres de los Caballeros, where his family was respected, though poor and untitled.

No mention is made of Balboa in the annals of the voyage, nor for years after the disbanding of the company at Santo Domingo do we find anything respecting the man who possessed those transcendent qualities that later marked him as a born leader of men. He was probably one of the unfortunates let loose upon the island when Bastidas was imprisoned by Bobadilla. At that time he was about twenty-six years of age, having been born in 1475. He was tall and robust, with a handsome, prepossessing countenance, and was one of the most expert swordsmen and archers in the island.

"His singular vigor of frame," says his Spanish biographer, Quintana, "rendered him capable of any degree of fatigue; his was the strongest lance, his was the surest arrow in the company; but his habits were loose and prodigal, though his nature was generous, his manners extremely affable."

He was, probably, just an average "soldier of fortune," and, finding Santo Domingo well suited to his tastes, took what came to him from his share in the voyage with Bastidas and spent it in riotous living. This one-time Indian Eden, or paradise, had been converted, by the passions of depraved men, into an abode fit only for the ruffian and libertine. With the farms and plantations assigned the new-coming settlers went large *encomiendas*, or slave-gangs, of unfortunate Indians, who belonged to their master utterly so long as they remained subject to his control. At the time of Balboa's advent the system was at its worst, for Bobadilla, knowing that his time was short, encouraged every Spaniard to make the most of his opportunities. Thus the poor Indians were worked beyond the limit of endurance, and died by thousands; thus the white men took to oppression as a matter of course, and became as fiends in human shape, with no regard for morals, for humanity, or the rights of their fellow-men.

Yet, with all the opportunities presumably given Balboa for acquiring a fortune, we find him, after several years in the island, deep in debt and seeking to avoid his creditors by flight. The first authentic notice of this former companion of Bastidas appears in a reference to him, in general terms, in the year 1510. At that time, four years after the death of Christopher Columbus, his only legitimate son, Don Diego, was governor of Santo Domingo and viceroy of the Indies. He had succeeded to the incompetent Bobadilla and the atrocious Ovando, who had left the island in such terrible condition that all his great energies were required to bring it under control.

Besides seeking to renovate the impoverished plantations and ameliorate the condition of the Indians, Don Diego also undertook the investigation of Santo Domingo's resources, and explorations in various regions of the Caribbean. He was especially interested in the development of Terra Firma, and encouraged expeditions thither, among them being the venture of Alonso de Ojeda, who, on one of his voyages, was accompanied by Francisco Pizarro, then unknown, but destined to become the conqueror of Peru. On his third voyage to Terra Firma, Ojeda left behind him in Santo Domingo one Martin Fernandez de Enciso, who was to follow after with a vessel freighted with supplies and reinforcements for a colony he had founded on the coast of Darien. It was on the occasion of Enciso's sailing that the reference, already alluded to, was made to Balboa and the class to which he then belonged: delinquent debtors who sought to evade their obligations by flight. Information having reached Don Diego, the admiral, that certain reckless men of this class meditated waylaying Enciso's ship when she called at some of the out-ports for final supplies, he issued a proclamation commanding them to desist from their purpose, and also sent an armed caravel with the vessel to escort her clear of the coast.

Vasco Nuñez de Balboa was then residing on a farm, which he nominally owned, near the sea-coast town of Salvatierra, at which place Enciso was to call for provisions. Indeed, some of the provisions were to come from Balboa's farm, and his own Indians were engaged in transporting them to the sea-shore. Late one afternoon, it is said, as Balboa and his *mayordomo*, or chief man, were walking on the sands near the mouth of the river that flowed through his farm, they saw Enciso's vessel and her escort standing into the bay. The sun was then not far above the western hills, beyond which towered the cloud-capped mountains of the interior, where lay the rugged region known as the Goldstone Country. The craft had scarcely furled their sails and dropped their anchors ere a puff of smoke shot out from the larger vessel, followed by the report of a cannon.

"Ha! that means haste!" exclaimed Balboa. "Bachelor Enciso is desirous that we send our supplies at once, so that he may lade to-night and sail to-morrow with the morning breeze."

"Well, master," said the mayordomo, "so far as our own provisions go, we are ready for him. These barrels on the beach, with what the Indians are now bearing hither on the road, make up our contribution to the cargo."

"Yes, Miguel," answered Balboa, "as thou sayest, we are ready. But, notwithstanding, there is one more contribution I fain would make to Bachelor Enciso's complement of soldiers, as well as add to his cargo. Dost understand me, Miguel mio?"

"I have heard, master, that thou art pressed for funds of late, and threatened with imprisonment provided money be not forthcoming for thy creditors."

"That is it. And dost know, Miguel, whence I may get that money—or, what is the same to me now, how I may evade payment for a while?"

"As to the *dinero*, master—'sooth, I know not where to find it; for if I did, certain thou shouldst have it. As to evading the payment, there is but one way open, and that—"

"Lies yonder," added Balboa, then continued, bitterly: "Yet it is not open, after all, for how can I get aboard the vessel? Don Diego—and may the devil get his soul in keeping, say I!—Don Diego has sent the caravel to prevent the escape of poor men like me who would redeem themselves in a far country. He would keep us here, it seems, to rot in misery, rather than afford us a chance to get gold for the payment of our debts."

"Don Diego is a fool!" exclaimed the mayordomo. "Yea, and so is the Bachelor Enciso. Faith, if we cannot outwit them both, thou mayst cut off my head and stick it on a pole! When canst thou be ready, my master?"

"In an hour, Miguel. But what will it avail?"

"Say no more, my master, but go to the rancho, and return to the beach within an hour or two. It were better if after dark; but not too late for getting aboard the ship."

"Oh no, not too late for boarding the ship," rejoined Balboa, derisively. "It hath ever been that, of late. But, what is thy scheme, Miguel?"

"Let not that concern thee, master. Go thou, and remember these proverbs: 'When the iron is hot, then is the time to strike'; and 'When the fool has made up his mind, the market is over!'"

Balboa laughed lightly as he hastened away to the rancho, whence he returned, two or three hours later, accompanied by an Indian porter with a full suit of armor on his back, and another with a large basket containing articles of wearing apparel.

Miguel was standing by a large cask, one end of which was open. Directing the Indians to deposit their burdens on the sand beside the cask, he sent them back to the rancho, thus leaving himself and Balboa alone. Not far away, though but dimly visible in the starlit night, a number of Indians were rolling casks of provisions into a small boat from the ship.

"They will be ready for this in about an hour," said the mayordomo, "so I fain must pack it quickly. What thinkst thou of thy quarters, master mine?"

"What? Is that thy scheme—to send me aboard packed like pork in a cask? Never, Miguel! The stigma would cling to me forever!"

"Not so closely, perhaps, as thy creditors, my master. But choose thou, and quickly, for time is no laggard. Meanwhile thou'rt making up thy mind, I'll pack this armor and clothing in the lower end of the cask. See, now, I shall secure it with braces, so the armor may not rattle; and observe thou that there are holes, which I have bored in the sides, to give thee air. Now, when quite ready, get therein, and I will head thee up, my master."

"But, Miguel, suppose the cask were to turn over? With the weight of my armor upon me, I should be suffocated, methinks."

"Nay, master, turned over thou shalt not be, for I shall give instructions to the crew to keep the top-end uppermost."

"But they may not observe them," groaned Balboa, as he clambered into the cask and settled himself in position.

"They will, master; trust me," said the faithful Miguel. "In the lading, they may roll thee about a bit, to be sure. Still, it will be better than to be squeezed by thy creditors."

"Well, as thou sayest, Miguel. In I go, perchance to a living tomb. A thousand ducats for thee, Miguel, if the venture prove successful."

"Ha! But when do I get it, master?"

"When I am lord of Terra Firma! But stay, Miguel. There is Leoncico. I cannot, must not, leave him behind."

"Truly thou sayest," replied the mayordomo; "but for the hound I have already provided. He goes aboard with Salvador Gonzalez, who, also, will have an eye on this cask, to open it at the proper time, which cannot be till to-morrow, know thou."

BALBOA CARRIED ON SHIPBOARD

"Ah, well! get me aboard; and caution the men to handle me carefully. *Adios*, Miguel, good friend. May the Lord reward thee."

Enciso's vessel was laden by midnight, and before dawn of the next morning was well in the offing, from the shore appearing a mere speck upon the horizon. The bachelor was now in high feather, for he had, as he thought, completely outwitted the scheming debtors of the island, who intended boarding his vessel, and had dismissed the armed caravel with a message to Don Diego to this effect. What, then, was his astonishment, about mid-forenoon of the first day out, to be confronted by a mailed apparition, in the person of the most notorious debtor that Santo Domingo had known—Vasco Nuñez de Balboa!

Clad in full armor, with his good Toledo blade in one hand and the famous hound, Leoncico, by his side, the soldier-colonist strode aft to the quarter-deck where Enciso was standing. He had been released from his cramped quarters in the cask by his neighbor Gonzalez, guided by Leoncico, who picked out his master's place of imprisonment from among the freightage in the vessel's bows, and stood by solemnly until he was freed.

"*Dios mio!*" exclaimed Balboa, after the head of the cask had been removed and his own head took its place. "That was an experience I would not endure again for an empire! Give me to eat, friend Salvador, and something to drink, for of a truth I am perishing of hunger and thirst. My limbs, too, are as stiff as a stake, so rub me down, *amigo*, and then help me on with my armor."

II

LEADER OF A FORLORN HOPE

1510

WHEN the Bachelor Enciso beheld Vasco Nuñez before him, even though the stowaway removed his plumed hat and bowed obsequiously almost to the deck, he was exceedingly disturbed. As he gazed, open-mouthed, upon the handsome countenance of Balboa, wreathed as it was with a most provoking smile, which seemed to say, "Aha! I have outwitted you at last," his choler rose, so that at first he could not find words for his wrath.

Finally it was voiced, and he poured forth, upon the still smiling vagabond in armor before him, a torrent of words which, since they were not chosen with a view to being reproduced for posterity to peruse, will not be repeated herewith. Suffice it that, when at last his rage and his vocabulary were seemingly exhausted, he was somewhat mollified by Balboa's single remark: "Well, Señor Bachelor, after all, the island, it seemeth, has lost a bad citizen, while you have gained a good soldier. Yea, two good soldiers, for here behold my hound, Leoncico, who will do more than one man's work, I ween."

"Scoundrel!" sputtered the lawyer, "what bad citizen—and, faith, you are one—ever became a good soldier? I have a mind—yea, a mind almost made up for that—to leave you on the reefs of Roncador, there to subsist on such as the sea may yield. And your impudence, moreover, to force yourself upon my company, when, as you cannot truthfully deny, you owe me, myself, two hundred ducats!"

"Nor do I deny it," answered Balboa, with a winning smile. "And the fact that I do not—and, moreover, seek you out—and, as you say, force myself upon your company—would not that imply that my motives are most honorable? Why should I seek to ally with one to whom I am indeed in debt but for a desire to liquidate that obligation? You yourself know, Bachelor, that there are now no opportunities in Hispaniola: none for the planter, even—which I am not; and scarce any for the soldier—which I am. Take me with you, then, and but give me opportunity. From the first spoils I win of the heathen, you shall recoup yourself the two hundred ducats, and I shall not rest until all my creditors have likewise been repaid in full."

"I do not know," remarked Enciso dubiously. "I remember the proverb, 'When the devil says his prayers, he wants to cheat you.' I never knew you, Vasco Nuñez de Balboa, to be over-anxious to discharge your debts. Still, since you are here, and if, before these men assembled, you will pledge your fealty, promising support and obedience to my commands, I will allow you to remain."

"I thank your excellency; and let me quote another proverb, which I verily believe in, '*Quien busca, halla*—He who seeks, finds!' I have sought, I shall seek yet more, and—I shall find!"

With these words, Balboa bowed low to the lawyer-captain, turned on his heel, and walked forward to rejoin his friends. Enciso looked after him, noting his stalwart, muscular figure, his independent poise, and shook his head. He had, indeed, gained a sturdy recruit, but one of such lofty and intrepid spirit that he might not be content with a position in the ranks, and, perchance, might some time aspire to command. Lawyer that he was, he was provoked to think that he had, in a sense, compounded with felony, and allowed a man to join his company who was under the ban of the law. But, like the lawyer that he was, he shrugged his shoulders and hoped all would turn out for the best. Balboa had his permission to stay, and even if he had not given it, he could not get rid of the impudent rascal without throwing him overboard.

Balboa joined his friends in the prow of the ship, and, with something of a swagger, told of his reception by Enciso, whom he complimented for his good sense in securing a good recruit, even though it had gone against his prejudices to do so. Salvador Gonzalez and a few other soldier-settlers, who had enlisted for the voyage and a year thereafter of service on land, then informed Balboa of the nature of the expedition in which he had engaged. They had turned the empty cask bottom up, and, gathered around Balboa's erstwhile domicile of the night before, regaled themselves upon viands brought from their Dominican farms. A goat-skin of wine hung conveniently near, and as this was frequently resorted to, the spirits of the company rose with the progress of the meal.

"You may not understand, Vasco Nuñez *mio*," said Gonzalez, "that this expedition we are on is for the relief of Don Alonso de Ojeda, who has made, now, three voyages to Terra Firma, and has founded a colony on the Gulf of Urabá. He and Don Diego de Nicuesa were given by the sovereigns permission to settle the coast of Terra Firma, between Cape de la Vela and Gracias á Dios, and they sailed from Santo Domingo, as you know, at or about the same time. When Don Alonso left, he had arranged with this our commander, the Bachelor Enciso, to prepare a vessel and follow him, after a certain interval. That interval has elapsed, and, true to his pledge, Don Martin Fernandez has set sail, and here we are, you see, on the high seas between Santo Domingo and the continent of mysteries [South America]."

"And well pleased am I," responded Balboa, "to find myself loose from that island of plagues and poverty. Whate'er betide, meseems we cannot do worse on the continent than in Hispaniola. Well it is that I preserved my good sword all these years that I have played the planter in that island, for now I see my way to carve a fortune with it in a new land where gold abounds. Here, then, is to the success of our voyage! May we find gold galore, and caciques as rich as was Caonabo when Don Cristobal Columbus came first to Hispaniola!"

He filled a calabash with wine, which he quaffed at a draught, and his companions likewise drank most heartily to the toast he proposed.

"How many are there in our company?" asked Balboa.

"One hundred and fifty men," answered Gonzalez, "plus yourself."

"Then there are one hundred and fifty-two, for Leoncico is as good as any soldier, and shall share on equal terms with all."

This Balboa said with such determination that it was easy to see his dog stood only second to himself in his estimation.

"Ay, he is a fine brute," assented Gonzalez. "I know him well. He is a son of Ponce de Leon's dog, Becerrico, who performed such feats in the island San Juan, and well worthy of his sire. And, inasmuch as Becerrico received a soldier's full share, yielding his master more than two thousand pesos in gold, as prize-money for those he captured, I see not why Leoncico should not be received among us on the same terms."

"You shall never regret it!" exclaimed Balboa, eagerly, "for on occasions he can render the service of a dozen men. He is a sentinel that never sleeps. By day and by night, he is ever on the watch. And, mates, his instinct is most wonderful. He can distinguish between a peaceful and a warlike Indian merely by his smell. When we were hunting down the Indians of the Cibao, ten Christians escorted by this dog were in greater security than twenty were without him. Seeing an Indian at a distance, I have loosed him, saying, 'There he is, seek him,' and he hath so fine a scent that not one ever escaped him. Having overtaken an Indian, he will take him by the hand or sleeve or girdle, perchance he have anything upon him, and lead him gently towards me, without biting or annoying him at all; but should the savage resist, he would tear him to pieces. Look at the scars upon him," added Balboa, proudly, drawing the blood-hound towards him and pointing out the many places where he had been wounded. "Most of these wounds were made by Indian arrows; but here is where a javelin struck and tore him badly, and here again where a spear glanced from his ribs that might else have penetrated to his heart. Ah, you are a great dog, aren't you, Leoncico?" The hound raised his massive head and sent forth a roar that resounded through the ship. He was an ugly brute, even for a blood-hound, and few aboard ship cared to handle him; but with Balboa he was like a kitten.

Pursuing a course southwesterly across the Caribbean Sea, Enciso's ship finally arrived at the harbor of Cartagena, where, as the Spaniards attempted to land, they were set upon by a host of savages, who had been roused to exasperation by Ojeda and were burning for revenge. Balboa and the more fiery of the cavaliers were for attacking them forthwith; but Enciso was of a peaceable disposition and would not consent. He withdrew from the shore a little way, and parleyed with the Indians through an interpreter, with the consequence that they desisted from their hostile demonstrations and soon engaged in friendly barter with the Spaniards. Though they had suffered severely at the hands of Ojeda, who had killed many of their warriors, women, and children, as well as burned their town to ashes, these so-called savages forgot their wrongs and mingled freely with the countrymen of those who had ravaged their territory.

Enciso took occasion to point out the advantages the Spaniards might always gain if they would treat these simple people fairly instead of with rank injustice, as was usually the case when the two races met. Balboa, Gonzalez, and their like, who had been schooled in the barbarous savagery of Bobadilla and Ovando, dissented from the bachelor's opinion, and declared he was altogether too lenient with the Indians. Then and there, in fact, began the dissension among the soldiers which resulted in Enciso's overthrow. But of that anon.

As they were about to leave Cartagena harbor, a sail was descried at a distance, which proved to be a brigantine laden with soldiers who had enlisted with Ojeda. This was proven to the satisfaction of Enciso, and on coming to close quarters he hailed them and demanded why they had deserted their post. He was answered by the commander of the ship, who was no less than the subsequently renowned Francisco Pizarro, that famine and savages had combined to drive them away. Ojeda, said Pizarro, had departed two months before, in a pirate ship bound for Santo Domingo, leaving him in command. He was to wait fifty days, and if at the end of that time no supplies or reinforcements came, was at liberty to abandon the settlement. The stipulated time passed, and the survivors of the wretched colony embarked in two vessels. One of these was swallowed by the sea, and the terrified crew of the other vessel sought the harbor of Cartagena, intending to sail direct for Santo Domingo.

They had endured enough, all agreed, having lost more than a hundred comrades by drowning, starvation, and the Indians' poisoned arrows. Even the indomitable Pizarro was convinced that a return to the deserted settlement was useless, for the savages had burned their fort before they left the harbor, and everything would have to be done over anew. But Enciso, as *alcalde mayor* by appointment of Ojeda, was then ranking officer of the little squadron, and Pizarro was subject to his authority. He yielded to his superior as gracefully as might have been expected in the circumstances; but soon after it was noticed that he and Balboa (having previously met in Santo Domingo, where they were at one time boon companions, in fact) had their heads together, and it was surmised, not without reason, that a plot was hatching.

The Bachelor Enciso was not devoid of tact, however, and to divert the malcontents led them on an expedition inland, to ravage the territory of the cacique Zenu and ravish the sepulchres of his ancestors, which were said to be filled with gold and gems. It was Balboa who related the story of the golden sepulchres, which he recalled as having heard when he was on that very coast with Bastidas.

"And, moreover," said he, "I bethink me of what was related respecting the gold of that region. It is said to abound in such quantities that it may be picked up by the basketful. In the season of rains, which is now, gold, in great nuggets large as eggs, is washed down by the torrents, and all the natives do to collect it is to stretch nets across the streams. Going to them in the morning, as a fisherman would visit his nets in the sea, they find the precious metal in such abundance that they bear it away by the backload."

Thus discoursed the redoubtable Vasco Nuñez de Balboa to his commander, Enciso; and though there were those on board ship who, knowing him of old, declared that he was prone to "shoot with the long bow," or, in other words, tell incredible yarns, the bachelor believed his story, every word, and prepared to put it to the proof. As he, Enciso, was a man of peace, more learned in the law than versed in the practice of arms, he allowed Balboa to take charge of the expedition, though he himself went along in an advisory capacity.

The remarkable abilities of the Bachelor Enciso shone forth in a remarkable manner at the outset, for, meeting with two caciques in command of a large army of naked warriors, he insisted upon expounding to them the "why and wherefore" of the Spaniards having invaded their territory. He had with him the old formula, drawn up by the learned doctors of Spain, which recited that, in virtue of the world having been given by God to the pope, and by the latter the unexplored regions of America to the king of Spain, hence the inhabitants thereof, which included, of course, those same Indian caciques, should submit to the Spaniards, etc. But these two caciques were strangely stubborn, for they could not perceive the connecting links in an argument which was supposed to be final as to the rights of the Spaniards to territory which they and their ancestors had held beyond the memory of any living man. One of them, in fact, was so rude as to inform the bachelor that while he assented to the proposition that there was but one God, who lived in the heavens, they could not understand how it was He had given the world to the pope, who also must have been drunk, or crazy, to present to the king of

Spain what did not belong to him. And he furthermore added that he and his friend were rulers over that golden province, and if Enciso persisted in his hostile action, they would be forced to cut off his head and stick it up on a pole. Then he and his warriors turned about and pointed to the palisaded fort behind them, where, over the gateway, ranged in grisly rows, Enciso and his men saw several heads that had once been carried on living shoulders.

This ghastly spectacle did not daunt Enciso, however, who said to Balboa and Pizarro, "Well, I have given them the law; now it only remains for you to give them what they can better understand, perhaps—that is, the sword and the lance."

The two dauntless fighters desired nothing better than the pretty fight that was promised with the caciques, and, with shouts to their followers, led them against the foe. The battle was short, but fierce. The two caciques were forced to retreat, leaving many of their men dead on the field; but two of the Spaniards were wounded with poisoned arrows, and died in torments. The province was ravaged, but no gold was found, either as ornaments in the sepulchres or nuggets in nets stretched across the roaring torrents.

III

BALBOA ASSERTS HIS SUPREMACY

1510

THE barren victory at Zenu did not serve to greatly strengthen the authority of Enciso, and it required all his arts as a solicitor to induce Pizarro's disgusted soldiers to return to San Sebastian—as Ojeda's settlement was called. It was situated on the east side of an inlet from the Gulf of Darien known as Urabá, the currents of which were so swift and strong as to force Enciso's vessel upon a shoal, where she went to pieces, with the result that nearly all her precious freight was lost, the men on board barely escaping with their lives. They reached the shore nearly naked and destitute, only to find their fortress and former dwellings in ashes, and the rapacious savages lying in wait for them in the surrounding forest.

A party sent by Enciso to forage the country was waylaid by Indians, who wounded several Spaniards with their poisoned arrows, and compelled the command to retreat to the shore. There a consultation was held, at which all present were unanimous for abandoning a region where, in their own words, "Sea and land, the skies and the inhabitants, all unite to repulse us." But they knew not whither to go, unless it were back to Santo Domingo, which, under the circumstances, would not be likely to receive them hospitably. At this juncture, the one man of that company who had less to expect from a return to the island than from remaining away from it, stepped forth and, by his words of encouragement, kindled in the hearts of the despairing colonists new spirits and new hopes.

"Now I remember," said Vasco Nuñez de Balboa, "that some years ago when passing by this coast on a voyage of discovery with Rodrigo de Bastidas, we entered this very gulf and disembarked on its western shore. There we found a large river, and saw on its opposite bank an Indian town, the inhabitants of which do not poison their arrows. The country adjacent, moreover, was open and fertile, so that, doubtless, we shall find there great store of maize and cassava, as well as a good site for a settlement."

This welcome information at once placed Balboa upon a pinnacle of prominence, and he was urged to lead the starving band towards the promised land of abundance. As many as possible crowded into the remaining brigantine, and sailed across the gulf, where they found the river and the town, just as Vasco Nuñez had described them. They landed at once and took possession, for the town was abandoned of its inhabitants, who had retreated to the forest. The place, however, was rendered untenable at the moment by its brave cacique, named Zemaco, who, with five hundred warriors, had intrenched himself on a near-by hill, where he courageously awaited the invaders, determined to give them battle. With such men as Pizarro and Balboa in his command, and the latter already aspiring to leadership, it was not possible for Enciso to restrain the ardor of his men, who would not heed his desire to parley with the Indians, but immediately attacked them in their chosen stronghold.

The Indians fought for their homes, but the Spaniards for their very lives, and with such desperation they battled that the issue was not long in doubt. The cacique and his warriors were driven from the hill with slaughter, and the victorious though famishing Spaniards, unable to pursue and overtake them in their flight, remained in possession of the town, with its ample stores of provisions and its treasures. They found in the huts, thrust beneath thatched roofs of palm leaves, many quaint ornaments of gold, such as anklets and bracelets, nose and ear rings, altogether to the value of ten thousand crowns. In the reeds and canes along the river, also, were discovered many precious articles concealed there by the Indians in their flight, and the cacique, having been captured and put to the torture, revealed the hiding-place of many more.

Thus suddenly raised from poverty to affluence, with more than twelve thousand pieces of gold in their possession, the Spaniards entertained hopes of acquiring yet greater wealth, in a short time, by marauding expeditions. But their ardent expectations were suddenly dashed by Enciso, who not only claimed the right to hold in his keeping all the gold, in conformity to royal command, but imprudently prohibited all traffic with the Indians on individual account, under penalty of death. As the greater part of his command was composed of men like Balboa, who had left their country in the hope of bettering their fortunes by barter with the natives of this golden region, dissatisfaction was wide-spread and the murmurings loud as well as deep. It was instantly perceived that the bachelor would prove a captious, miserly master, and the bolder spirits of the company resolved upon resisting his authority.

All had agreed, meanwhile, that the Indian village was well situated for a permanent settlement, and, after sending for the remainder of his company at San Sebastian, Enciso commenced to lay the foundations of a town which, in fulfilment of a vow he had made, he called Antigua del Darien. He was the founder of the town of Antigua, but was not to remain long in control of it, for, having without sufficient force to back him attempted to restrain the passions of his followers and deprive them of their liberties, he was soon to be swept away when those pent-up passions burst their bounds.

The Spaniards of those days had a deep reverence for royal authority and fear of their king; but when it was casually discovered that Enciso had unwittingly settled upon territory which had been granted to Nicuesa, and over which neither Ojeda nor himself had any jurisdiction, he was promptly deposed by the soldiers, who refused him further allegiance. He was beaten by his own weapons—those of the law—which were turned against him by his chief opponent, Balboa, who had never forgotten Enciso's threat to throw him into the sea, or land him on a desert island, when he had first made his appearance on shipboard. The line of demarcation between the territories granted to Ojeda and Nicuesa respectively ran through the centre of the Gulf of Urabá, the eastern shores of which pertained to the former and the western to the latter.

As Antigua had been founded on the western shore, it undoubtedly lay within the limits of Nicuesa's grant, and hence the unfortunate Enciso was without a legal leg to stand on. "This miser who would deprive us of our gold," said Balboa, "and who covets for himself all the fruits of our efforts, would use to our prejudice an authority to which he has no just claim. Placed as we are, beyond the limits assigned to Ojeda's jurisdiction, his command as alcalde mayor is become null, together with our obligation to obedience."

Enciso could not refute this argument, and was set aside, in his place being elected as alcaldes, or magistrates, Vasco Nuñez de Balboa and a man named Zamudio. Though the majority of the company had chosen these two as their chiefs, there were still some discontented ones, and finally the altercations became so violent as to threaten the disruption of the little colony. In the midst of it, one day, as the disputants were hotly engaged in the market-place, they heard the sound of cannon and saw signal-smokes arising from the hills across the gulf from Antigua. They replied in like manner, with cannon and smoke-signals, and soon two ships were seen sailing from the eastward, which, on arrival in the river, proved to be in command of one Diego de Colmenares, who had come from Spain in search of Nicuesa, the long absence of whom without tidings had excited alarm.

Learning that opinion in the colony was divided as to the authority that should rule there, Colmenares agreed to remain and share his arms and supplies with the colonists, provided they would receive Nicuesa as their leader. This proposition having been acceded to (for the liberality of Colmenares had gained him universal favor), he and two others were deputed to go in search of the lost leader, who, with seven vessels and five hundred men, had disappeared, months before, and left no sign by which others could follow him. It was known that he had taken part with Ojeda in an attack upon the Indians at Cartagena, after which he had set sail for his allotted territory to the westward of Urabá. Since then nothing whatever had been heard from Nicuesa, but the search of Colmenares disclosed the details of a terrible narrative of suffering and fatal disasters, almost without a parallel in the annals of exploration. In short, at the time Colmenares set out from Antigua, only sixty men survived of the five hundred who had sailed from Spain with Nicuesa, and but one brigantine was left of his fleet.

The unfortunate explorer was finally found at a port on the north coast of the isthmus named Nombre de Dios, where he and the remnant of his band were existing in a state of utter despondency, unable to get away, and despairing of assistance from any quarter. This port had been discovered and named by Nicuesa himself, who, on reaching it when worn by fatigue and exhausted by hunger, had exclaimed: "En nombre de Dios—in the name of God—let us rest here!" There he and his companions gave up their battle against the elements and hostile savages, and in the apathy of despair awaited the end. From this situation they were rescued by the coming of Colmenares, who snatched them from the very jaws of death.

This Nicuesa had been a man of some distinction in Spain, where he had held the office of royal carver, and had amassed quite a fortune. He was just such a vivacious and testy cavalier as Ojeda himself, with whom, by-the-way, he came near fighting a duel over their respective boundaries. His reckless and generous disposition was made manifest by the bountiful dinner he ordered prepared from the stores brought by his rescuer, at which he proudly exhibited his skill as a carver, by slicing and disjointing a fowl while held in the air on a fork. His imprudence was shown by repeated boasts that he would promptly chastise those who had ventured to question his authority over Antigua, and would take from them all the gold of which, without his permission, they had possessed themselves. It belonged to the crown, he said, and to him, and those who held it must disgorge, even to the last *centavo*, which he would force them to do immediately on his arrival. Colmenares and his two companions were disgusted, and their apprehensions were further excited at the story told them by one Lope de Olano, who had formerly come to Nicuesa's relief, and had been imprisoned by him on a technical charge of desertion. "Take warning by my treatment," he said, privately, to the envoys. "I brought relief to Nicuesa, and rescued him from certain death when starving on a desert island; but behold my recompense! He repays me, as you see, with imprisonment and with chains. And such, believe me, is the gratitude the people of Darien may look for at his hands."

Colmenares continued loyal to his chief, but his companion envoys, Corral and Albitez, were so impressed by the avaricious disposition displayed by Nicuesa, that they hastened ahead of the brigantine in which he embarked, and, arriving at Antigua before him, warned the inhabitants against receiving the boastful ingrate into their midst. "A blessed change we shall make," they said, "in summoning this Diego de Nicuesa to take supreme command. We have called in King Stork with a vengeance, and he will not rest until he has devoured us. What folly is it, being our own masters, and in such free condition, to send for a tyrant to rule over us!"

Their words, indeed, produced a turmoil, and the two parties of Enciso and Balboa, though opposed to each other, quickly united in opposition to the landing of Nicuesa. When the man without a government arrived in the river opposite Antigua, the people sallied forth as if to receive him, but with loud cries and menaces warned him against disembarking, and ordered him back to Nombre de Dios. It was a desperate situation for Nicuesa, who felt, indeed, as if "the heavens were falling on his head." To be warned away from his own territory was humiliating, but to be sent back to the isthmus meant death by starvation. He entreated, then, to be allowed to land, though merely as an equal and companion; failing in that, he begged the heartless Spaniards to take and imprison him, since, though he should lose his liberty, his life might be saved thereby. But the factions were obdurate, and when, in spite of Balboa's warning, Nicuesa persisted in landing, a band of vagabonds pursued him along the shore until, by sheer fleetness of foot, he escaped from them and plunged into the forest.

At sight of this once respected cavalier, who had lost a fortune in his expedition, and was now reduced to the extremity of flight before a rabble crew, Balboa's heart misgave him. He had been foremost in exciting the populace against Nicuesa, but he had not expected such a tempest of disapproval as to threaten his life, and strove earnestly to allay it, though in vain. His fellow-alcalde Zamudio was the most demonstrative against the poor wretch, fearing to lose his position should he be allowed to assume the government. One of his most zealous supporters was a burly ruffian named Benitez, who was so vociferous that Balboa, after repeatedly warning him to desist, suddenly set in motion the machinery of the law, and, in his capacity of magistrate, ordered him to receive one hundred lashes on the bare shoulders. This act of lawful violence cooled the emotions of the mob somewhat, and poor Nicuesa was allowed to emerge from the forest and seek shelter on his brigantine. Here he received word from Balboa that his only safety lay in keeping out of sight aboard the vessel; but the next morning, while his friend's attention was attracted in another direction, he was lured on shore by a deputation assuming to have been sent to treat with him, and hastily cast into a small and unseaworthy vessel, which was set adrift upon the waters of the gulf. Together with seventeen comrades, who chose to accompany him on his perilous voyage, Nicuesa was thrust into the miserable craft, which, with scant provisions and little water, was sent forth to cross the Caribbean Sea, and was never heard of again.

Nicuesa was thus disposed of the first week in March, 1511. He was never to return; but a few years later his avengers exacted reparation for this barbarous deed, and Balboa lost his life partly in consequence. After ridding themselves of Nicuesa, the Antiguans resolved upon sending Enciso after him, and under form of the law succeeded in doing so. He was, however, better equipped for a voyage than his lamented predecessor, and in the caravel which conveyed him to Santo Domingo and Spain went also the alcalde Zamudio. He had been prevailed upon by his partner to take the voyage for the purpose of presenting their cause at court, and thus, at a single *coup*, the wily Balboa removed an enemy and a rival from the colony, and was left in sole and absolute command.

IV

BALBOA CAPTURES A PRINCESS

1511

UNTIL the expulsion of Enciso, says a Spanish writer of the century in which the actions narrated occurred, Balboa might have been considered as a bold and factious intriguer who, aided by his popularity, aspired to the first place among his equals, and who endeavored, artfully and audaciously, to rid himself of all who might, with better title, have disputed it with him; but as soon as he found himself alone and unrivalled, he gave himself up solely to the preservation and improvement of the colony which had fallen into his hands. He then began to justify his ambition by his services, to raise his mind to a level with the dignity of his office, and to place himself, in the scale of public opinion, almost in comparison with Columbus himself.

The removal of the colony from San Sebastian to Darien had been done in pursuance of his advice, and the wisdom of this act being apparent to everybody, he was thereby raised above all others in the estimation of his companions. He was not made giddy by his elevation to supreme power, but, on the contrary, seemed sobered by it, as though he realized his responsibilities, and also wished to justify his comrades' confidence in him. Having been invested with the command, he became a real leader and actual head of affairs, always first in any toil and danger, and shrinking from no exposure, whether to the elements or the weapons of the savages. While frank and affable in common discourse, and ever accessible to the meanest and most humble colonist, yet he was a strict disciplinarian with reference to his soldiers, and insisted upon being treated with the deference due him as governor-general of the colony and captain of its forces. He fully recognized the necessity for collecting ample supplies of gold, to be forwarded to King Ferdinand of Spain, in order to purchase exemption from punishment for his expulsion of Enciso, a royal official; but he deprived no man of his portion in consequence. Balboa was probably one of the most generous and high-minded of the Spanish-American conquerors. While he sometimes treated the Indians with barbarity, and his exactions bore heavily upon them, yet he was never unfair to his comrades when it came to a division of spoils. He was known to have relinquished his own share on more than one occasion, in order that his followers might not lose their reward for the toils and dangers of an arduous campaign.

Having united the warring factions among the colonists, and secured the unswerving loyalty of his soldiers by offering them in himself an exemplar of soldierly qualities, Balboa turned his attention to establishing the colony on a basis of thrift and security. He built a stockaded fort, repaired the dilapidated brigantines, ordered extensive fields to be cleared for planting with corn, and drilled his soldiers constantly. No tidings coming from the exiled Nicuesa as the weeks went by, Balboa despatched vessels for the rescue of whatever survivors might be discovered at Nombre de Dios and along the intervening coast, thereby saving several half-starved wretches from death. Among others thus rescued were two Spaniards who had fled from the severities of Nicuesa more than a year before, and found refuge with the cacique of a province called Coyba. They were nearly naked, like the Indians, and their skins were painted, after the fashion in vogue among the savages; but they could still speak their native language, and thenceforth served Balboa as interpreters. They had been kindly treated by Careta, the cacique of Coyba, who had freely given them shelter, food, and clothing; but their first thought, when they found themselves safe at Darien, was how they might betray him and assist their countrymen to obtain his treasures. Shown into the presence of Captain Balboa, they eagerly offered to lead him to Coyba, where, they said, he would find an immense booty in gold as well as vast quantities of provisions.

"And this cacique Careta, you say, treated you well?" he asked.

"As well as he could, being a savage," answered one of the men. "He is naught but an Indian, half the time going naked, and with manners not of the best; but such as he had he freely gave us, and saved us both from death by starvation, most likely."

"And yet," rejoined Balboa, with a curl of his lip, "ye would have me attack this generous chieftain, lay his town in ashes, perchance kill him and some of his subjects?"

"We have naught against him," answered the man, evasively; "but, being possessed of gold, of which he knows not the use, and of provisions, which ye certainly need in this settlement, it seemed to us our duty to acquaint you with these things."

"And that was well," exclaimed Balboa, "for of a truth we need both gold and supplies for our larder, which is low, even near to being exhausted. As to gold—indeed, as you say, the savage knows not its value, while to us it is the greatest and best thing in the world. We are already under ban of the king, most probably, for hastening the departure of the Bachelor Enciso, and unless I can persuade his majesty, with a golden argument, of the justice of our doings, it may go hard with me and with us all. So now, as I say, this news comes most opportunely, and peradventure it turn out to be true, ye shall not suffer for the imparting of it. I will myself lead the way, with you as guides, and if we can accomplish our object without bloodshed, much better will I be suited than if violence be done."

Balboa was highly elated by the tidings of a golden country not far distant, and, selecting a hundred and thirty of his best men, embarked them in two brigantines for the province of Coyba. They were equipped with the best weapons the colony could supply, and also with utensils for opening roads into the mountains, as well as with merchandise for traffic should it seem better to barter with the Indians than attack them openly.

The swamps and forests adjacent to the colony were occupied by Indians of different tribes, some more warlike than others, but none of them so barbarous as the fierce Caribs of the eastern shore of the Urabá Gulf, who ate their prisoners, gave no quarter in battle, and made use of poisoned arrows. These terrible weapons, as already remarked, were not used by the Indians of the western shore, who were far less sanguinary, though obstinate in battle and even ferocious. They spared the lives of their captives, and, instead of eating or sacrificing them to their gods, branded them on the forehead, or knocked out a tooth, as a sign of servility, and kept them as slaves. Each tribe was governed by a cacique, or supreme chief, whose title and privileges were hereditary, and who was permitted to have numerous wives, while the common warrior had but a single helpmeet, unless he had won unusual distinction by great bravery in battle. Besides supporting their caciques, the Darien Indians allowed priests, or magicians, and doctors to exercise their arts, and they adored a supreme deity, known as *Tuira*, to whom the milder tribes offered spices, fruits, and flowers, while the more savage ones poured out blood upon their altars and made human sacrifices.

VILLAGE ON RIVER OF DARIEN

The houses of these people were mostly made of poles, or canes, loosely bound together with vines, and roofed with a thatch composed of grasses and palm leaves so thickly placed as to turn the tropical rains and afford a perfect shelter. When these structures were built on solid ground they were called *bohios*, as in the islands of the West Indies, and some of them were nearly a hundred feet in length, though not over twenty or thirty in breadth. The majority, however, were small huts, at a distance very much resembling hay-stacks, having a single opening only, as a doorway, and a clay or earthen floor, with a fire usually burning in the centre, the smoke from which escaped through the roof of thatch. There was another class of dwellings, either aerial or aquatic, depending upon whether they were built in trees, for safety from floods and wild beasts, or above the placid surface of some lake or gulf, and used as dwellings by fishermen. These were known as *barbacoas*; and it is worthy of note that we find the same name applied to certain elevated structures of a similar sort used as corn-cribs by the Indians of Florida in De Soto's time. Both bohios and barbacoas were subject to removal or abandonment whenever the game of the neighborhood grew scarce, the soil unfruitful, or a pestilence decimated the tribe, following the dictates of danger or necessity.

During the greater part of the year, in that tropical climate, clothing was rarely necessary for warmth, except at night, and the men and boys were nearly always naked, though the caciques sometimes wore breech-cloths, and cotton mantles over their shoulders as badges of distinction. All males, and especially the warriors, painted their bodies with ochreous earths, and stained their skin with the juice of the annotto, while they adorned their heads with plumes of feathers. Both sexes inserted tinted seashells in their ears and nostrils as "ornaments," and encircled their wrists and ankles with bracelets of native gold. The women, after reaching the marriageable age, wore cotton skirts from waist to knee, and broad bands of gold beneath their breasts. Their hair, which was very coarse and black, they cut off in front, even with their eyebrows, by means of sharp flints, but allowed the thick, luxuriant tresses to fall over their shoulders as far as the waist.

They were fine-looking people, especially the young girls and children, for, though their complexion was brown, or copper-colored, their forms were models of symmetry, their countenances pleasing, and their dispositions sweet and amiable. Their defects (for they were by no means devoid of them) were such as might be expected to arise from their barbarous mode of life, descended from ancestors who had never been instructed in morals or religion, save in their most brutish forms. They had, of course, no written language, nor even a hieroglyphic system, to perpetuate their thoughts or the traditions of their ancestors; but they were experts in the chant and dance known as the *areito*, which they performed to the rude music of drums made of hollowed logs, like the *tambouyé*, or "tom-tom," of the Africans.

Free from the cares of civilization, their occupations agricultural, with frequent forays into the forest for game and upon the river and gulf for fish, they passed much of their time in idleness, except when pressed for hunger or incited by passion to war upon their neighbors. They knew not, as has been said, the value of gold, for they were always willing to barter great nuggets for the veriest trifles and toys; but Careta, the cacique of Coyba, may have been instructed in its worth by the two Spaniards who had shared his hospitality, for when, under their guidance, Balboa appeared in his settlement and demanded his treasures, he declared he had none to supply. Neither had he any provisions, he said, except such as were necessary to carry his tribe over to the next planting season, for he had been engaged in a disastrous war with Ponca, a powerful cacique who lived in the mountains, and his people had been unable either to sow or to reap.

Then one of the traitors took Balboa aside, and said:

"Commander, believe him not. To my certain knowledge, he hath an abundant hoard of provisions in barbacoas concealed in the forest, and of gold, also, vast quantities hidden in the reeds and thickets. But it is best to dissemble, for behold, he is surrounded by two thousand warriors, and they will fight, as I know from having seen them combat with the tribe of Ponca. Appear to believe him, then, and pretend to depart for Antigua; but in the night return, take him by surprise, burn the village, and make the cacique prisoner, with all his family."

This advice seemed sound to Balboa, and he acted on it promptly, turning about that afternoon and making as though departing for Darien, after a cordial leave-taking, to the cacique's great delight. The unsuspecting chieftain watched the Spaniards out of sight, heard their drums and bugles resounding through the forest farther and farther away, and, convinced that they had indeed left him in good faith, retired to rest without setting scouts on their trail or posting sentinels about his camp. But the sagacious Balboa had no sooner placed a league or so of forest between himself and the unwary Careta than he ordered a halt. The wood was dense and dark, for the trees of the tropical forest are not only vast of bulk, but thickly held together by innumerable vines and bush-ropes, called *lianas*, seemingly miles in length, and forming impenetrable bulwarks, overtopped by canopies of foliage, through which the sun even at mid-day can hardly send a single ray.

Having with him, however, axes and *machetes* for cutting his way through the forest, the prudent Balboa had commanded his men to slash a broad path ahead of the company, and thus, when they halted for rest shortly after sunset, behind them lay an open, easy trail leading directly back to the cacique's village. After posting sentries roundabout the camp, Balboa ordered a bountiful meal to be served his hungry men, one hundred of whom were allowed to sleep for the space of two hours, after which the command was given to march.

Without bustle or confusion, the soldiers formed in loose order and commenced their retrograde march through the forest, thanks to the foresight of their commander, finding the return far easier than the advance. All was silent as they approached the village, and, as stealthily as jaguars about to leap on their prey, crept within bow-shot of the dwellings. Balboa had passed the order for his men to refrain from shedding blood, unless a fierce resistance were offered, and, whatever happened, to capture the cacique and his family alive. The royal dwelling was conspicuous from its size and its position on a mound raised somewhat above the general level of the town, and it was silently surrounded by a picked company.

Suddenly the twang of a cross-bow string broke the stillness of the night, followed by a sheet of fire from an arquebuse; for two of the soldiers had spied some Indians moving through a thicket, and concluded the whole village was alarmed. At once, in terrible confusion, from the surrounded houses outpoured swarms of startled savages, naked and weaponless, seeking security by flight, and with no intention of resisting the unexpected attack. Several of them were cut down by the swordsmen and halberdiers, and a few were transfixed by arrows from the cross-bows; but the greater number were allowed to dart into outer darkness and escape. Nearly all escaped, in fact, except the cacique's numerous family, who, surrounded by the soldiery, with naked swords and lighted fusees in their hands, cowered around their dwelling in affright.

One alone attempted to escape, and would have succeeded but for Leoncico, Balboa's faithful hound, who had effectively assisted at "rounding up" the band, and was keeping a vigilant watch at his master's side. With a leap and a growl, Leoncico sprang over the heads of the group in front of him and disappeared in the darkness of the wood. "Dios!" exclaimed Balboa, in alarm. "It was a woman—a maiden! God grant she may not resist him! I never knew Leoncico to harm a woman, but he has torn many a man to pieces. Gonzalez, take you command for the moment, while I follow the hound to see that he does no harm to the maiden." Saying this, he plunged into the wood, which grew close up to the cacique's dwelling, and with his sword and heavy armor cut and beat down the vines that stretched across the path his hound had taken. Soon he was surrounded by silence, as well as by darkness, for the Indians who had fled to the forest lay quiet, like hares in a form, and the turmoil of the village was left far behind him.

"Leon—Leoncico!" he shouted, "where art thou?" For a while there was no response, then a hoarse bark sounded in his ears. It came from a point well ahead, deep in the wood, but by dint of sword and armor he forced his way to it, and there found that of which he was in search. The darkness was intense, for the time was then about midnight; but as he pushed his way onward a stray gleam of moonlight thrust a lance-like shaft through the leafy canopy above, and he saw the form of Leoncico crouching in front of a cringing figure outlined against the trunk of a mighty tree. Then Balboa drew breath with great relief, for, despite the darkness, he could see that the captive was, apparently, unharmed. She was pressed close against the tree-trunk, clinging for support to a sturdy liana, and motionless, save for the trembling which shook her like a leaf.

She seemed, indeed, a statue cast in golden bronze. Fear had paralyzed her limbs so that she did not move, even when, approaching softly, Balboa called to her to be of good cheer and touched her reassuringly. She continued gazing at the hound with wide-staring eyes and parted lips, as though fascinated by that terrible apparition. She had never seen its like before, and could not but have been bereft of sense and motion when it had sprung upon her from the darkness of the forest, like a phantom of evil.

Realizing that his errand had been accomplished with the appearance of his master, Leoncico rose with a growl, and would have returned to the village had not Balboa halted him. "Lie down, brute," he cried, in a voice hoarse with rage. "What do you mean by pursuing a defenceless maiden? Were there not warriors enough for you to slay?"

The hound cringed before him and whined, as though to exculpate himself; but suddenly his whole attitude changed. Springing erect, and thrusting his nose into the air, while the hair on his neck bristled with rage, he uttered a low, deep growl. At the same instant the whistle of an arrow came to Balboa's ears and a missile struck him forcibly between the shoulders. But for his armor he might have been transfixed, so forcefully was the missile-weapon sent; but, as it was, it fell in fragments to the ground.

Then there was the sound of a scuffle, a shriek of agony pierced the air, followed by the ravening of Leoncico as he tore to pieces the victim of his rage. He had sprung upon the savage who in the darkness had approached and sped the arrow at his master, and, bearing him to the ground, made short work of the poor wretch, who was soon a mangled corpse. Stupefied as she was by fear, the maiden could not but have felt the horror of that terrible scene, and sank senseless to the ground. War's dread experiences had not so seared the heart of Balboa that he could be insensible to pity for his helpless captive, and, sheathing his sword, he gathered her in his arms. Preceded by

Leoncico, he bore her tenderly through the forest, shielding her from harm in the darkness, and in due time joined his command at the village.

V

THE CACIQUES OF DARIEN

1511

AS Vasco Nuñez burst into the circle of light shed by the flames of burning bohios, the red glare from which lighted up the steel-clad soldiers and their abject captives, he was greeted by glad exclamations from the former and cries of distress from the latter. He strode through the lines without a word, and, making for the group containing the cacique's family, he sought out an elderly female, whom he supposed to be the mother of the girl, and delivered his charge into her keeping. The cries of distress were instantly hushed as the happy mother gathered the girl in her arms, but as the minutes went by without any signs of recovery from the maiden, low moans broke from the captives, and many of them began to gash themselves and tear their hair.

The cacique had stood aloof, stoically refraining from uttering a sound; but after a while, as his daughter did not return to consciousness, he went to the side of Balboa, and, raising his manacled hands in the air, exclaimed:

"What have I done to thee, O thou terrible stranger, that thou shouldst treat me so cruelly? None of thy people ever came to my land that were not fed and sheltered and treated with loving kindness. When thou camest to my dwelling, did I meet thee with a javelin in my hand? Did I not set forth meat and drink, and welcome thee as a brother? Set me free, therefore, with my family and people, and we may yet remain as friends. We will supply thee with provisions and reveal to thee the riches of this land. But first restore to me my daughter, the light of my eyes, the pearl of my household, whom thou and that dread beast of thine have driven to the borderland of death."

During this impassioned speech by the outraged cacique, Balboa remained gazing first at the chieftain, then at his daughter, without uttering a word. The mother was chafing the wrists, bathing the forehead, and whispering tender words into the ears of the maiden, but without eliciting a response. A most pathetic spectacle mother and daughter presented, despite the savagery of the parent, her lack of clothing, and uncouth appearance, which but enhanced by contrast the beauty of the maiden.

Balboa had thought her beautiful, in the brief glimpses afforded in the moonlit forest, but now, with her form and features wrought upon radiantly by the flickering flames, he saw that she was ravishingly lovely. Touched by her beauty, then, and rendered compassionate by her helplessness, he allowed his heart to go out to her, and so far as his rough nature was susceptible to love he felt that sentiment for the cacique's daughter. Distressed by the silence with which his appeal had been received, the cacique added:

"Dost thou doubt my faith? Behold my daughter. I give her to thee, provided she shall be restored, as a pledge of friendship. Thou mayst take her for thy wife, and be thus assured of the friendship of her family and her people."

Balboa then awoke, as from a trance, and, grasping Careta's right hand, exclaimed: "I accept her, if she will but ratify thy offer, and henceforth there shall be no enmity between us. Men, cast off the chains from these people. Set them free; and bugler, order the recall, peradventure there be any in pursuit of our former enemies, now our friends."

With his own hands he removed the manacles from Careta's wrists, then, noting by the flickering of the maiden's eyelids that she was recovering, he hastened to her side. As her eyes opened, they rested in astonishment first upon the mailed cavalier, standing erect in the firelight, clad in shining armor from throat to foot, and with a smile upon his handsome features.

Then in the fulness of his manly powers, with a face and figure that would have wrought havoc among the dames of his sovereign's court, had he been favored with a presentation there, Vasco Nuñez de Balboa carried this untutored maiden's heart by storm. She uttered a low cry, and, leaping from her mother's lap, darted into the cacique's dwelling, as if for the first time realizing her lack of proper raiment and desiring to conceal herself from the eyes of her lover. At a word from the cacique, whose will was law with all his family, the mother went in after her and soon reappeared, holding her daughter by one hand. During the brief time at her disposal, she had found and arrayed herself in a flowing robe of cotton, embroidered in gold, and gathered at the waist by a golden girdle. This she clutched nervously, as, with dejected mien and downcast eyes, she stood before the man in whose sight she had found favor above all other women.

The marriage ceremony was simple and brief, consisting in the cacique's joining the right hands of these two so strangely brought together, and invoking his deity to bless the union, which, at a later period, Balboa intended to have sanctioned by a priest. Whether this intention was fulfilled, we will not at this moment inquire. Balboa was a man of many good resolves and promises, most of which seem to have been made only to be broken. But, in the sight of God, who sees into the souls of men, and in the presence of more than one hundred witnesses, who looked on in vast astonishment as the ceremony was performed, Vasco Nuñez de Balboa was "well and truly wedded" to the cacique's beautiful daughter. She, the simple child of nature, untaught by art, and with no moral law to guide her, knew and cared for naught except that she loved the gallant cavalier and sought no further.

BALBOA AND THE INDIAN PRINCESS

Short and fierce had been the wooing of the fair Cacica, wild and weird the accessories of her wedding, with the accompaniment of burning dwellings and attendance of rude soldiers in armor bearing flaming torches. Brief and tempestuous was to be her life on earth thereafter. Balboa may have reckoned upon this alliance as attaching to his service one of the most powerful caciques of Darien; but by captivating the affections of the beautiful Cacica he had incurred the hatred and jealousy of certain young warriors, who were to cause him trouble in the near future. He had captured the wild beauty of the wilderness, but in so doing he enmeshed himself in troubles of far-reaching consequence. They reached, indeed, across the sea and ocean even to Spain, and in their train brought retribution, none the less certain because it was delayed for years.

Love and diplomacy went hand-in-hand, so far as Balboa could perceive, and as few men ever succeed in reconciling these two, he affected to believe that he had achieved a victory of great moment. Returning to Darien with his bride, he there entertained his friend and father-in-law with jousts and tourneys, showed him the ships, and surprised him with the thunder of artillery. Nothing delighted, as well as alarmed, the old chieftain so much as the war-horses, upon the back of one of which he was mounted, only to be thrown heavily to the sands and receive a rude awakening. He then conceived an intense admiration for the beings, like his son-in-law, who could mount and control those wonderful animals, and never tired of sounding their praises. As he had disclosed to Balboa the hiding-places of his provisions and treasure, and as the latter had lost no time in transferring them to Darien, he was instrumental in keeping starvation from the colony until supplies arrived from Spain or Santo Domingo, and also of enriching every man in the army. Two brigantines had been laden with the provisions and spoils obtained in Careta's territory, in the securing of which the lovely Cacica was largely instrumental. She induced her father to reveal to her new master the treasure-vaults amid the sepulchres of her ancestors; but when she witnessed the rapacity and brutality of the conquerors in ravaging the graves and desecrating the revered remains, she was grieved to the heart. Perhaps she then had a foreboding of the evils she was to bring upon her people, for she became pensive and sad, rarely smiling or singing during several days thereafter. Upon the warriors of the tribe the ravage had a different effect, rendering them surly and restive, so that the cacique was hardly able to restrain them from making reprisals, and avenging the indignities offered their ancestors by shedding the blood of the Spaniards.

The attachment of these people to the memory of their dead caciques and former rulers is shown by the fidelity of their wives and servants, who immolated themselves upon their graves, in order that they might continue to serve them in the next life as they had done in this on earth. They fully believed, says the old chronicler, that "the souls which omitted this act of duty either perished with their bodies or were dispersed in air. They consigned their dead to earth, though in some provinces, as soon as a chieftain died he was seated on a stone, and, a fire being kindled around him, the corpse was kept till all moisture was dried, and nothing but skin and bones remained. In this state it was placed in a retired apartment dedicated to this use, or fastened to a wall, adorned with plumes, jewels, and even robes, by the side of the father or ancestor immediately preceding. Thus, with the corpse of the warrior, was his memory preserved to his family, and if any of them perished in battle, the fame of his prowess was consigned to posterity in the songs of the areitos."

Shortly after the return of the cacique to his village, Balboa missed his mistress one day, and, setting scouts on her trail, traced her to the Indian cemetery. His emissaries had strict orders to bring her to him at once, if they found her; but they returned empty-handed, and when he rated them for disobedience one of the scouts replied: "Señor Comandante, had you seen what we have seen, you yourself would not have taken the Cacica from her people. For she and they were engaged in paying honors to the dead, whose tombs we have, in their opinion, desecrated by robbing them of their jewels. All the warriors of her father, the cacique, were gathered around the cemetery, armed with weapons and painted as if for war. Sooth, they were fierce and warlike, and it needed but a small provocation to kindle the flames of their resentment into a blaze that might sweep this colony into the sea. They had gathered the bones of their deceased rulers together and reinterred them carefully, those who were dried like mummies by heat having been affixed against the walls whence they were wrested by our soldiers. When we arrived—and, truly, we dared not enter the place, but hovered unseen on the verge of the forest—they were engaged in various ways. The women and younger folks were singing and dancing their barbarous areito, performing steps in unison to the beat of a drum made from a hollowed log with the skin of a jaguar stretched over one end of it. It was a strange, unearthly sound, and reverberated through the forest like the roll of distant thunder. The warriors, in a circle apart and enclosing the whole, were drinking deeply of fermented liquors, produced from the palm and the maize, which ever and anon they shared with the dancers. This they would do, we were told, until all had drunken themselves into a frenzy, and the dancers became exhausted from fatigue and drunkenness combined. Judge, then, O Comandante, if we should have been justified in attempting to bring away the cacique's daughter, thy mistress and spouse."

"And she was there, also? Was my Cacica there, performing in those horrid ceremonies so barbarous and so vile?"

"Truly was she, one of the foremost in ladling out the liquor and entreating the warriors to drink. But, so far as we could observe, she did not herself partake thereof. Nor did she allow, nor was there offered her, any indignity; but great respect seemed accorded her, as the daughter of the chief."

Balboa groaned in spirit, but his pride forbade him making audible comment on the strange proceedings of his bride. Another day he waited, expectant of her coming; but he did not remain idle meanwhile, since, having little faith in the friendship of the cacique, he ordered out all his men-at-arms and prepared to receive the savages with fire and sword, provided they should rouse themselves to frenzy and attack the settlement.

Nothing of a disturbing character occurred, however, and when, on the evening of that day, Balboa sought his hut, worn down with fatigue and sorely perplexed in his mind, his still beloved Cacica came forth to greet him. How she had come he knew not, nor did he ever discover, though the settlement was surrounded by sentinels specially charged to watch for and detect her presence. Like a spirit, or an invisible bird of the night, she had flitted through the cordon of sentinels and gained her house without being detected by one of them. They declared afterwards, one and all, that she must have been in league with the powers of the air and, presumably, evil—endued of the devil—to have accomplished this feat. But none durst say a word of this to their commander, for he was still infatuated with the beautiful princess—sure token, the soldiers affirmed among themselves, that she was a witch, for whom burning at the stake might be too mild a punishment.

However Vasco Nuñez may have been vexed by this misadventure of his beloved, he gave no sign of it, or, if he did, was soon soothed by her blandishments into apparent forgetfulness. But in the minds of both had been begotten a distrust that was destined to work havoc with the good understanding that should ever exist between people situated as were they. Soon after, seeming confidence was restored between the settlers and the Indians, who came and went as formerly, bringing provisions from their gardens, which they exchanged for knives, beads, and toys from Spain. They gained access to the settlement as simple traffickers, intent on adding to their store of trinkets and trifles; but Balboa divined that they had other incentives, in fact, and came as spies. Still, he did not allow his suspicions to become apparent to Careta, with whom he had formed an offensive and defensive alliance for their mutual protection.

In the mountains resided a cacique already mentioned named Ponca, a rival and adversary of Careta, who wished the Spaniards to join with him in an invasion of his territory. There was no immediate necessity for the Spaniards to make war upon Cacique Ponca, as he had not offended them in any particular, nor were they in need of a further extension of territory, since the valley they had occupied, situated between the sierras and the cordillera of the Andes, was extremely fertile and capable of sustaining a great number of inhabitants. It was not only excellent for planting, with rich soil and abundant natural resources, which came early to perfection beneath the ardent sun of the tropics, but abounded in game, while its rivers and the bordering gulf teemed with fish in great variety.

But the Spaniards were less inclined to agriculture than to war, and would rather ravage their neighbors' territory for gold than extract from the fertile soil the products it so generously yielded to the cultivator. Had they been less covetous and restless, less avaricious and rapacious, they might have avoided contact with the ferocious tribes of the interior, and perhaps have prospered.

There was, however, an unseen force at work constantly against them which they could not successfully combat. This was the climate, which made terrible inroads upon the health and constitutions of the Spaniards, by the great heat and humidity of the air, and the heavy, almost incessant rains, which came down at times as plunging torrents.

Nothing less than the most unquenchable ardor and the most marvellous resolution, says the historian, could support the Spaniards under so many discouragements and overcome so many difficulties. Perhaps it was because they possessed this ardor in an excessive degree that they continually panted for fresh conquests and desired to come into conflict with the savages. Their great incentive, as already remarked, was the acquisition of gold, and, learning that Cacique Ponca possessed the precious metal in abundance, they were easily induced to join with Careta in an attack upon him. Taking his troops by sea to the point nearest to Ponca's capital, Balboa marched rapidly upon the village, which, finding it deserted, he sacked and burned. He obtained considerable booty, to which his ally, Careta, laid no claim, being content with having humbled his adversary and driven him still farther into the mountains, whence Ponca sent messengers imploring a cessation of hostilities.

Having "pacified" the country, Balboa was for returning to Darien, but was persuaded by Careta to diverge to his own province, where he was royally entertained by the cacique. The latter had a neighbor, one Comogre, who was yet more powerful than himself, having about ten thousand Indians under him, three thousand of whom were warriors. His province comprised an extensive plain and beautiful valleys, situated at or near the foot of a very lofty mountain, which rose far above the general altitude of the cordillera, or backbone of the isthmus. Messengers sent by Comogre guided Balboa to this province, in the capital of which the cacique awaited his coming. As the Spaniards approached, Comogre came out to welcome them, attended by a train of sub-chiefs, and followed by a vast number of his subjects. Included in his suite were seven stalwart young men, his own sons by as many different wives, of whom he was inordinately proud. Each son had a habitation of his own, but that of the cacique surpassed anything of the sort the Spaniards had seen in the land, for it was "an edifice of an hundred and fifty paces in length and fourscore in breadth, built on stout posts, surrounded by a lofty wall, and on the roof an attic story of beautiful and skilfully interwoven woods. It was divided into several compartments, and contained its markets, its shops, and a pantheon for the dead, where the dried corpses of the cacique's ancestors were hung in ghastly rows."

These corpses were in a retired and secret part of the structure, says the historian, set apart for that special purpose. The bodies had been dried by fire (as already narrated in the account of Careta's ancestors), so as to free them from corruption, and afterwards wrapped in mantles richly wrought and interwoven with pearls and jewels of gold, and with certain stones considered precious by the Indians. There they hung about the hall, suspended by cords of cotton, and were regarded not only with reverence, but apparently with religious devotion. The Spaniards gazed upon them in amazement, not unmingled with a burning desire to despoil this hall of fame and secure for themselves its wonderful treasures.

VI

FIRST TIDINGS OF THE PACIFIC

1512

CACIQUE Comogre's sons were young men of whom any father, savage or civilized, might have been proud, but especially distinguished for his intelligence and sagacity (says the Spanish biographer of Balboa, Señor Quintana) was his eldest son, who was also his father's favorite. He took note of the glances exchanged by Balboa and his lieutenant, Colmenares, when they were inspecting the pantheon, and rightly construed their meaning, which was, of course, that they would give much for the privilege of sacking the place and depriving the sacred dead of their rich ornaments. He had been informed of what had taken place in his neighbor Careta's province, and knew that neither the opposition to their rapacity of argument or force, nor any consideration for religion or the dead, could restrain them were they to conceive the desire to ravish the sepulchres of his ancestors.

His father had three thousand warriors, ferocious and reliable; but, from what he had been told by Cacique Careta, who had tasted their quality and tested their valor, they could not stand for an hour before the two hundred Spaniards then in his province. The mailed men, Careta said, would scatter them like chaff, and, with the fire from their muskets and cannon, devour them as the flames consumed the grass of the plains. Then he conceived the idea of purchasing exemption from ravage by bribing the commanders, in the hope that by so doing they would refrain from desecrating the tombs he held in such regard. But he did not know, what he was later to learn, that the more the Spaniard obtained the greater grew his appetite, and that by displaying the wealth of the land he was but hastening its ruin. Simple son of Comogre! He had, then, much to learn.

After consulting with his father, who was elated that a son of his should possess such sagacity and penetration, the young cacique sent for Balboa and Colmenares, who met him in the great square of the town. "Great and worthy ones," he said, "here are sixty slaves, male and female are they—all are yours, to be divided between you as may seem desirable to both. And here, great and worthy ones, are golden ornaments, taken from the hoard saved by our fathers. To us they are of use only as mementos of the dead, for to the accumulation of riches we are not given, being content with what we can eat and what we need to protect us from the elements. We give you these things freely, because we see that you value gold above all else, and because we would find favor in your eyes and desire your friendship."

Balboa and Colmenares were at first overcome with astonishment, but when they recovered speech they thanked the cacique and his son in extravagant language—and then began to quarrel over the division of the treasure. The slaves were of some account, but the chief treasure consisted in the gold, which, when they had weighed and carefully estimated its value, was found to amount to four thousand crowns. Most of it was in the shape of animals of various sorts, and must have caused the native artisans great labor; but of this the avaricious Spaniards took no account, and all went into the melting-pot, greatly to the grief of the young cacique.

Having always the fear of his sovereign in mind, and the potentiality of gold to buy the king's favor, Balboa first set aside a fifth part for royalty, which was to be despatched to Spain at the first opportunity. Then he attempted to divide the remainder between himself and companions; "but this division begat a dispute that gave rise to threats and violence, which, being observed by the high-minded Indian, he suddenly overthrew the scales in which they were weighing the precious metal, exclaiming: 'Why quarrel for such a trifle? If such is your thirst for gold that for sake of it you forsake your own country and come to trouble us in ours, I will show you a province where you may gather it up by the handful—yea, and carry it off by the backload!'"

When, by a blow of his fist, the spirited savage had overturned the scales and scattered the gold on the ground, the Spaniards standing by were greatly enraged; but when his speech was finally translated to them they were exceedingly astonished, and desirous of learning more respecting that golden province of which he told them.

QUARREL FOR THE GOLD

"Where is it?" demanded Balboa and Colmenares, in a breath. "Show us the way, and we will follow you at once."

"Nay, nay," answered the young man, with a shake of his head. "It lies beyond those lofty mountains, far to the south. Beyond them, again, extends a mighty ocean, a glimpse of which may be gained from the mountain-peaks, but it is many days distant to the west and the south. To succeed in getting there, you should be more numerous than you now are, and will need at least a thousand men, even though with coats like those you have on, which neither spears nor arrows can pierce. For you will have to contend with powerful kings, who will defend their dominions with vigor. You will first find a cacique who is very rich in gold, who resides at the distance of six suns from here. Climbing the mountains, ever climbing, climbing, you will reach their summits, and then behold the sea, which lies in that part." And he pointed to the south. "There you will meet with people who navigate in barks with sails and oars, not much less than your own in size, and who are so rich that they eat and drink from vessels made from the metal which you so much covet."

This was the first information conveyed to the Spaniards of the Pacific Ocean and Peru, and they were vastly excited over it, endeavoring to get the young man to furnish them further details of the country intervening, as well as of the great sea, its extent and situation.

"Go back to your settlement," continued the young cacique, "there to prepare for a journey of many days. Select your stoutest and bravest soldiers, and provide them well with food and weapons. Then return to us, and we will furnish you guides. My father's warriors will go with you; but of yourselves, as I said, you should be a thousand strong—no less than that—for we shall meet hosts of warriors, some of them cannibals, who eat the flesh of men, and all of them fierce fighters, such as those of the cacique Tubanamá, in whose province is gold beyond measure. Stay, I will send for one of my men who was once a captive to Tubanamá, and he will tell you the same."

The quick-witted cacique had seen distrust lurking in Balboa's eyes, and, indeed, the Spanish commander conceived this might be but a scheme to get him out of Comogre's country and into the mountains, where he might be swallowed up in the wilderness and never return to the colony, which would be attacked by the Indians and destroyed. But the former captive of Tubanamá, who was questioned separately from the young cacique, confirmed the latter's story in every particular, and verified his account of gold which might be found in all the streams, as well as accumulated in the cacique's treasuries.

Then Balboa, says one who was near him and saw the journal he wrote with his own hand, was transported by the prospect of glory and fortune which opened before him. He believed himself already at the gates of the East Indies, which was the desired object of the government and the discoverers of that period. He resolved to return, in the first place, to Darien, to raise the spirits of his companions there with these brilliant hopes, and to make all possible preparations for realizing them. He remained, nevertheless, yet a few days with the caciques, and so warm was the friendship he contracted with them that they and their families were baptized, Careta taking in baptism the name of Fernando, and Comogre that of Carlos. Balboa then returned to Darien, rich in the spoils of Ponca, rich in the presents of his friends, and still richer in the golden hopes which the future offered him.

Darien was in sore straits when, elated with his several victories, Balboa marched into the settlement at the head of his little army. Notoriously improvident as they were, the Spaniards had planted, notwithstanding, a large tract with maize, or Indian-corn, and were looking forward to gathering a harvest, when down from the mountains swept a torrent, accompanied by a tempest with thunder and lightning, and in an hour their fields were totally ruined. Starvation stared them in the face, but about this time the *regidor*, Valdivia, who had been sent to Santo Domingo by Balboa, with gold for Diego Columbus, returned in a small vessel well laden with provisions.

These stores were soon consumed, and Valdivia returned to the island, bearing a rich present for Don Diego and fifteen thousand crowns in gold for King Ferdinand. This amount of gold, it was estimated, was due the sovereign as the royal fifth, which was exacted from all treasure obtained in America. As there was frequent communication between Santo Domingo and Spain, and as, moreover, Don Diego Columbus was viceroy over the islands, and Terra Firma as well, it was proper and politic to send the treasure by the hands of the admiral. The latter had sent abundant promises of aid, but, though Balboa represented that it was necessary for him to have at least a thousand men as a reinforcement, it is not on record that he ever got them. He had in mind the invasion of the country contiguous to the great sea, which, Comogre's son had told him, would demand more than a thousand soldiers, fully armed and equipped. Failing to interest Don Diego in the scheme, Valdivia was instructed to sail from Santo Domingo for Spain and lay it before the king, who, in view of the large amount of gold remitted, might feel inclined to accede to his modest request.

Valdivia sailed from Antigua del Darien, bearing with him the king's fifth, and charged with Balboa's message, which was emphasized by a startling statement that unless the needed troops were despatched without delay, he should be obliged, in self-defence, to exterminate all the caciques on the isthmus. He had already, he wrote, slain thirty caciques, mainly with his own hand, and "must in like manner destroy every one he should capture, as the small number of his troops left him no alternative." We may probably take this message as evidence, rather, of Balboa's skill with the "long bow," already alluded to, than of the slaughter he committed with more potent weapons, for he certainly possessed a vivid imagination.

Valdivia, the regidor, sailed for the island and Spain, but was never heard of more, and it is probable that his ship went down with all on board. With him, also, went the fifteen thousand pieces of gold, besides other sums, sent by Balboa and his men to satisfy their creditors in Santo Domingo. Truly, an evil genius pursued him, he was prone to say, for, labor as he might, he could not make head against his adverse fortune. Greater opportunities were given him, perhaps, than to any man then living since the days of Columbus, and it cannot be truly said that he did not improve them to the utmost; but every great endeavor of his came to naught. He was ardent and generous, and he was sane, save where his passions were concerned. His command over men was a marvel to all who knew him, and there was not a soldier in his command who would hesitate to follow him anywhere. He never told his men to go, but always asked them to *come*, for he was ever in the forefront of battle, and the more desperate the enterprise, the more anxious was he to take part in it and assume the leadership.

Life in the settlement irked him greatly, says his Spanish biographer, and although it was essential to its peace and prosperity that he should stay in it a certain length of time, in order to place the town in a posture of defence and encourage the waning spirits of the settlers, his active and enterprising disposition would allow him no rest. He had desired to go in person to present his cause to the court, but his fellow-settlers would not hear of it. They were already sadly distressed by their losses, through the inimical effects of the climate and the repeated attacks of the Indians, and there seemed to be no one but Balboa who could hold them where they were. What they had really gained was very little, since their harvests were washed away by the floods, and the gold they had acquired was useless, without marts in which to purchase the things they most required to sustain life.

In order to keep them from seizing a vessel and departing for more attractive regions, Balboa conceived the plan of invading the dominions of Dobaybe, which lay around the head of the gulf, and contiguous to the cannibal country on its eastern boundary. He was obliged to await the return of Valdivia with reinforcements, if he would invade the great and opulent region beyond the mountains, but meanwhile there came to him information of a character that fanned to a flame the slumbering desire to achieve a great discovery. An Indian was brought to him one morning, who said he was the subject of a great cacique living in a golden realm of the interior about one hundred miles from Darien. Its capital was situated on the bank of the very river that emptied itself, by many mouths, into the Gulf of Urabá. Its riches were prodigious, and it derived its name from a wondrous goddess of most ancient times, who, according to Indian tradition, was the mother of the god who had created the sun, the moon, and the stars. She also controlled the elements, he said, sending great storms, with thunder and lightning, which destroyed the habitations of those who did not worship her fervently, but rewarding those who did with abundant crops and success in battle. According to some, this goddess had been at one time an Indian princess, whose capital was in the mountains of Dobaybe, and in whose memory, after her death, a temple had been erected containing a golden idol, which was still worshipped by the natives. Both temple and idol were made of gold, and to the holy shrine it was the wont of Indians far and near to make annual pilgrimages, for the purpose of making offerings of their wealth. Thus, in the course of centuries, the golden temple had become filled with treasure of inestimable value. Its walls were adorned with plates of gold, and its vaults filled with the precious metal, veins of which radiated from them to the various mines with which the region abounded.

The idol and the temple were of themselves sufficient to arouse the predatory instinct of the Spaniards; but not alone was their cupidity appealed to, for Balboa was informed that his old enemy Zemaco had retreated to the province of Dobaybe, and was engaged in arousing its cacique to resistance. Inflamed, then, by a lust for gold and their desire for revenge, the followers of Balboa volunteered so readily for the desperate enterprise that he had difficulty in retaining any able-bodied soldiers for the defence of the settlement. One hundred and seventy were finally selected, and embarking them in two brigantines, under command of himself and Colmenares, Balboa sailed up the gulf to the mouth of the river draining the golden country.

While nothing more was ever heard of Balboa's friend, the regidor, yet tidings indirectly came to the Spaniards, in the course of Cortés's voyage to Yucatan, in the year 1519. When his fleet was off that coast, a rumor reached him that two Spaniards were held captive by a cacique of the interior. One of these was rescued, and proved of inestimable value to Cortés in the conquest of Mexico, as an interpreter. His name was Aguilar, and he informed his rescuers that he and another were the only survivors of the shipwreck, all the rest, thirteen men and two women, having been sacrificed, or killed by hard usage.

VII

A SEARCH FOR THE GOLDEN TEMPLE

1511

NOTHING seemed impossible to the Spaniards of Balboa's time, nothing seemed incredible, and thus it was that this small band of soldiers set forth in full confidence that they could subdue any force they might encounter, and trustfully accepting the wild story told them by the Indian. They were the pick of the force at Darien, the hardiest and stoutest-hearted, and they were armed with the best weapons known to their age. These weapons, indeed, were not such as would satisfy a soldier of the present day, for, besides pikes, swords, lances or halberds, and cross-bows, they had as a fire-arm only the rude arquebuse, or clumsy musket, which was a heavy burden to carry and rarely did effective execution. It was so heavy as to demand a "rest," or support, which was usually afforded by a pronged upright of iron, or a crotched stick; and besides being difficult to properly charge with powder and ball, it required the musketeer to carry constantly a lighted match, or fusee, with which to ignite the powder in the pan.

Most soldiers preferred the powerful cross-bow, with which the best of them could drive nails almost as far as they could see them. But these weapons were not so far superior to the bows possessed by the Indians that they gave their owners great advantage, and besides, the savages were generally more powerful of arm than the Spaniards, as well as equally expert with bow and arrow. The chosen weapon of the Spaniard was the sword, and the cavalier who possessed a good "Toledo," with blade that could be bent double without breaking, and with an edge that nothing could turn, considered himself more than the equal of any warrior that might oppose him, whether armed with bow, spear, pike, or war-club.

The vast superiority of the Spaniards over the savages consisted in their armor, for protected as most of them were, by helmet, corselet, gauntlets, cuishes for the thighs and greaves for the legs—arrows, spears, and even war-clubs glanced harmlessly from their panoply of steel. They were often wounded, some of them killed outright, in their desperate encounters with the Indians; but the greater number of their casualties were the result of carelessness or neglect to properly encase themselves in defensive armor. Heavy and cumbersome as it was, few men could support the weight of metal it was necessary for the armed soldier to carry, and especially in the tropics was the burden found intolerable. So it happened frequently that the soldiers were surprised by the savages without their armor, which they may have doffed for temporary relief, or have delivered over to a slave to carry for them. At such times there was found to be little difference between savage and civilized soldier, and the former fought his opponent on nearly equal terms.

Balboa may have taken with him a few falconets, or light field-pieces, but if so they were not used in conflict with the Indians on this enterprise, and the prestige which the white men had derived from their fire-arms was maintained by the arquebusiers, or musketeers, who frightened the Indians with the loud reports of their guns and volumes of sulphurous powder-smoke, but did little execution. The commander himself carried as his only weapon his invincible sword, the blade of which had been forged at Toledo, and brought to an exquisite temper in the waters of the Tagus. For defence he relied upon the armor in which he was encased, and the Saracenic shield, or buckler, which hung from his shoulders or was carried on his left arm, the right wielding the basket-hilted sword.

When Balboa reached the river, which came down from the mountains far away, he knew not which branch of it to take, there were so many mouths, and all navigable, so far as he could see. Taking his stand in the prow of the brigantine, he guided his little fleet into the largest stream he could find, and then, sending Colmenares to explore another branch, he proceeded on his way to what he thought was Dobaybe province. After threading his way through a perfect labyrinth of morasses, and without getting a glimpse of a single Indian, he at last came to a deserted village. The huts were empty, containing neither inhabitants or provisions; but hanging from their rafters were many jewelled weapons and golden ornaments, so that the Spaniards obtained booty from this silent village to the estimated value of seven thousand castellanos. This they stowed away in two large canoes, which had been picked up along the river-bank, and then, discouraged at the gloomy outlook, Balboa gave the order to return to the gulf. On the way a violent storm assailed these invaders of the country ruled by Dobaybe's deity, sent, the trembling Indians said, in revenge for this affront offered her by the unbelieving white men. The brigantine was in such danger of sinking that half her cargo was thrown overboard, to save her, while the two canoes laden with the booty were overwhelmed by the waters of the gulf and went down with all on board.

Thus far the expedition had proved worse than fruitless; but Balboa was not the man to cry "enough" until every means had been exhausted to gain what he was seeking. The river he had entered, and which he had the honor of discovering, was far greater than he imagined, for it has its source, say the geographers, nine or ten hundred miles distant from the Gulf of Urabá, in the cordilleras of the Andes. The volume of its waters was such as to freshen the sea for many leagues from the shore. It was named by Balboa the St.

John, but is now known as the Darien and the Atrato. Working his way into the branch of the river ascended by Colmenares, Balboa overtook his companion, and together they entered a tributary of the main stream which, from the color of its waters, they called the Rio Negro, or Black River. Its color was derived, they ascertained, from the black mud of a submerged region through which it ran, and where they discovered the most wonderful habitations of any seen by the Spaniards since Vespucci and Ojeda brought to light the lake-dwellers of Maracaibo, in 1499.

As the brigantines were slowly forced against the current of the river, now beneath the overhanging branches of huge trees swarming with parrots, and again crossing the placid surface of an eddied lake, the excited soldiers caught occasional glimpses of large animals ahead climbing the trunks of trees. At first they took them for monkeys, and those of the band who had cross-bows got them ready to shoot; for the flesh of the monkey was held by them in great repute, and their supply of meat was exhausted. Suddenly one of the soldiers, who had climbed to the mast-head for better observation, cried out: "Those are not monkeys, but men! They are men and women and children; and behold, there are their barbacoas, like nests, perched up in the palms above the water!"

And it was as the soldier had said, for there was a veritable nest of tree-dwellers, or rather a collection of nests, consisting of wicker-work huts made of flexible reeds and vines, fifty or sixty feet up in the air. They occupied the tops of the palm-trees, and each was large enough to accommodate a family, being divided into compartments, such as bedchamber, dining-room, and kitchen, or larder. They were reached by ladders made of split reeds or bamboos, which the Indians climbed with the agility of monkeys. Women and children, as well as men, went up and down the fragile, shaking ladders, some of them with great burdens on their backs, with as little inconvenience as if they were walking on level ground.

All their provisions were kept in the aerial houses, which were well filled, but the liquors they drank, consisting of palm-wine and beer, were buried in earthen jars at the roots of the trees, as the rocking of the habitations would cause them to become turbid. The trees grew in or near the water, and the Indians kept canoes tied to their trunks, or to the lower ends of the ladders, and thus could embark without touching the earth. Their mode of life, in fact, was aerial and aquatic, rather than terrestrial, for they perched in the trees like birds, and sported in the water like fish, upon which latter they almost entirely subsisted. They rarely hunted the big game of the forest, and their chief reason for living up in the trees was that it afforded them security from wild beasts, especially the jaguars, which nightly roamed the woods in search of prey.

Balboa was greatly diverted by these barbacoas up in the air and their agile inhabitants. He endeavored to capture some of the latter, but they were too spry for him and his clumsy companions in armor, for, before they succeeded in landing, every member of the community was safely ensconced aloft. After the frightened Indians had scampered up the ladders they drew them into the tree-tops also, and, considering themselves secure, began to pelt the Spaniards with stones. This was more than their leader could endure, and, sheltering himself behind his buckler, he advanced to the tree in which, as he was told, the cacique's hut was built, and demanded that he descend immediately. The only answer was a shower of stones, some of which struck his shield, and one of them, glancing, wounded a companion. Becoming then enraged, Balboa ordered an arquebuse to be fired into the tree, and when the cacique, whose name was Abebeiba, heard the loud report and saw the cloud of smoke ascending, as from a volcano, he nearly fell from his lofty perch.
"Hold!" he cried, "I will descend"; but when his wives and family entreated him not to do so, he wavered, and finally refused to budge.
"What have I done to thee?" he asked of Balboa. "In nothing have I offended thee and thine; now leave me in peace."
The grim commander said nothing in reply, but commanded his axemen to attack the tree. "When the old scoundrel sees the chips fly," he remarked, "perhaps he may change his mind." Protected by the soldiers with their shields, the axemen vigorously set their blades into the palm-tree, and then the cacique seemed disposed to capitulate. Down rattled the long ladder, and it had scarcely struck the ground ere the cacique was there beside it, shaking with fear and chattering like a parrot. After him also came his wives and their children, in a long and rapidly descending procession, and soon they were grouped around the palm-tree, which, by their swift compliance with Balboa's demand, they had saved from destruction.

"We want gold," said Balboa, threateningly. "If you have any up in that tree, go back and get it at once."

The cacique replied: "I have no gold in the tree nor in any other place. I have no occasion for gold; but, great lord, if you will allow me to search in yonder sierras, I will soon return with a vast quantity, for there it exists and I know its hiding-place. Behold these wives of mine and these sons; they will be hostages for me against my return."

"It is well," answered Balboa. "Go, but return within two days. Meanwhile, we will hold your family as hostages, and enjoy the provisions you have so bountifully supplied against our coming, as it seems."

The wily Abebeiba departed for the sierras, and the Spaniards watched him out of sight. They saw him cross the river in his canoe, then plunge into a thicket on the opposite bank; but they saw him no more, for he never came back.

VIII

CONSPIRACY OF THE CACIQUES

1512

BALBOA waited three days for the return of the cacique, with his brigantine, meanwhile, moored in a bend of the stream, where the dense vegetation of the banks met in leafy arches overhead. Great trees, their roots in the earth of opposite banks, mingled their verdant crowns together, and over their trunks (as though formed by nature for this purpose) climbed the natives of the region when they wished to cross the stream. One of these arboreal giants bent above Balboa's brigantine, with its branches screening the deck so effectually that the soldiers were nearly always in refreshing shade, even with the sun shining brightly at noonday.

The heat of that region was intense, and a shade was ever grateful, so it was with feelings of disgust that the sailors and soldiers heard Balboa, one day, give the order to proceed up the river. They had become attached to the spot containing the palm-trees and the dwellings in the air, for the habitations afforded them pleasant retreats when off duty, and their occupants received them with smiles and offers of good cheer. Balboa and his officers had taken possession of a group of huts consisting of the cacique's and others, nestled together in a clump of palms hung with great bunches of nuts and flowers amid their leafy crowns. There their hammocks were hung, there they were waited on by nut-brown boys and maidens, who took them fruits and beverages, the latter so often that soon the big earthen jars at the roots of the trees were drained of their contents.

It was when apprised of this fact that Balboa decided he would proceed with the exploration. "By all the saints!" he said to Colmenares, as the two reclined lazily in their hammocks, watching the smoke-wreaths drifting upward, mingled with most appetizing odors from their breakfast simmering in earthen vessels on the fires beneath the trees. "By the saints, Rodrigo, this is a pleasurable life to lead!"

"*De veras*—Of a truth," answered Colmenares. "But, my commander, have we not other things than pleasure to consider?"

"As thou sayest, Rodrigo, we have. And, now the *chicha* is gone, the jars are empty, and the temptation removed for the old cacique to indulge in drunkenness—peradventure he ever return, which I doubt—it seemeth to me we had best move on."

It was not often that Balboa allowed himself to relax, as he had done here, especially when in the enemies' country, and his conscience smote him. Then he gathered himself together and gave the order which produced such discontent among his men. He met their sour looks blithely, giving them no heed, and they were too well trained to oppose him, even for a moment. Such as were by duty compelled, bent themselves to the oars, while others cast off the moorings, and soon the brigantine was on its way again up the stream. Just as it was slipping out from beneath the overhanging trees, there was a sudden commotion in the vines and branches above the deck, and through the tangled mass of vegetation dropped a naked savage. He was evidently a warrior, for in one hand he grasped a bow and bunch of arrows, and in the other held a shield of jaguar-skin.

"Ha, what is this?" exclaimed Balboa, who was standing on the castle-deck directing the departure. "Ho, there, interpreter! Come hither. Surround him, men, and prevent him from escaping."

There seemed, however, no cause for alarm, as the warrior was alone and showed no evidence of an intention either to attack the soldiers or leap overboard. As Balboa approached him, drawing his sword from its sheath the while, he stood like a statue, and faced the oncoming soldier without flinching.

"Ask him whence he comes and what the object of his coming," said Balboa to the interpreter, who, with others, had hurried to the spot.

The warrior did not at first reply to the question, repeated by the interpreter, but, after gazing about defiantly, finally made answer: "I come from the cacique Zemaco, who hath a prisoner in his possession, one of thy kind, whom he will set free and deliver to thee provided thou wilt send for him. But not many must thou send, only two or three, whom I will guide to his camp."

"A prisoner? How comes he to have a prisoner?" demanded Balboa, looking around for an answer. "We have lost no man, of late. I misdoubt the story myself, and believe the Indian is lying."

"And I likewise," said Colmenares. "But let us find from him where the cacique is encamped. Where is Zemaco?" he asked the warrior, through the interpreter.

"At Dobaybe," was the answer. "He guards the great temple and its goddess of gold."

"Aha!" exclaimed Balboa. "Then we will go to him. But not with an embassy; in force will we go. How far is it to Dobaybe? Ask him, interpreter?"

"Two days direct, by land; but four days by river, in the big canoe," answered the savage, showing his teeth with a snarl of rage, like a jaguar glowering from a tree in the forest.

"That time he told the truth," said Colmenares.

"So far maybe as he hath told anything," replied Balboa, enigmatically. "My faith! but I've a mind to put him to the torture. If it be but two days to Dobaybe, then surely we can accomplish it; but if much more, we shall be obliged to return for provisions. Where is the armorer? Here, man, place this savage in irons!"

As the armorer approached, Balboa waved his hand towards the Indian, who, probably divining the fate in store for him should he linger, sprang for the rail. At one bound he reached the bulwark, at another he leaped over it into the water of the river, where he sank like a stone before the astonished witnesses could make a move to prevent him. Instantly there was a commotion aboard the brigantine. A score of soldiers hastened to the rail, and as many cross-bows were made ready and levelled at the surface of the water. If the head of the savage had appeared above it, surely it would have been pierced by several bolts from the bows; but it did not emerge. The impatient bowmen waited long, but in vain. The Indian was seen nevermore, for he probably swam under water to the thickets on the farther shore, and, worming his way through the vines and undergrowth of the forest, secured his safety by flight.

"Maria Santisima!" exclaimed Balboa. "Why did I not run him through with my sword? He was a spy—naught else was he; and all that he told was a lie!"

Downcast and disgusted were the soldiers then, for they felt that they and their commander had been outwitted, and by a naked savage. "If, then," they reasoned among themselves, "we can be so easily deceived by an emissary of Zemaco, what cannot he do to us when involved in the net he has spread for our capture?" They were ignorant and superstitious. Having heard of the goddess that reigned in the mountains, and having experienced her might, as shown in the tempest she had, without doubt, visited upon them, they were prone to ascribe to her the possession of supernatural powers, and balked at the prospect of invading her territory. If the truth were told, Balboa himself was not without a trace of that same superstition, and he could understand the feelings of his men, if he did not, indeed, sympathize with them. When, therefore, at the end of a week of fruitless quest, wandering in the forest and seeking in vain a conflict with the fugitive Zemaco, he found himself back at the point of departure on the Rio Negro, he for a time gave up the hunt and abandoned his search for the golden goddess and temple.

The unsolved mystery of the idol and temple continued to vex the Spaniards for many a year. When an indomitable soldier like Vasco Nuñez de Balboa found himself frustrated in the search for them, few others had the courage to take it up. It was not like Balboa to retire and acknowledge himself defeated, and it was much against his will that he turned his back upon the unseen Dobaybe and set his face towards Darien again. He did not, however, abandon the project utterly, and gave a pledge that he would sometime return, by leaving behind a body of thirty soldiers, under command of Bartolomé Hurtado, who were to hold the country in subjection. They took possession of a deserted village on the Rio Negro, and, while Balboa with the main body descended the river to Darien, ranged through the country in pursuit of fugitives.

From what afterwards transpired, it would seem that Cacique Zemaco had been playing a game of deep duplicity with his more civilized opponent, and, whether he held possession of the golden Dobaybe or not, had some sort of a stronghold in the mountains to which he could retreat on occasion, and which Balboa had not been able to reach. As soon as the latter's back was turned, he descended from his stronghold, and spread his warriors along the rivers, retaking the deserted villages and collecting their inhabitants together.

When Hurtado and his little band were left alone in the wilderness, Zemaco perceived an opportunity for revenge upon the Spaniards; but he was cautious and had a wholesome fear of their weapons. He waited until Hurtado had detached more than half his total force, for the purpose of taking their prisoners to Darien, and then launched his bolts of war. Hurtado's captives were placed in a large boat guarded by fifteen or twenty Spaniards, most of whom were invalided through wounds or sickness, and thus scarcely ten sound men remained behind in the Indian country. The boat descended the Rio Negro very slowly, for it was heavily laden with its human freightage, and late one afternoon, when between forest-covered banks that closely approached and cast a gloom upon the waters, it was attacked by Zemaco and his warriors. They were in four canoes, and were armed with war-clubs and lances. Shouting their war-cries, they surrounded the boat containing the Spaniards, and with the assistance of the prisoners massacred all save two. These two escaped by leaping into the river and clinging to the trunk of a great tree which was floating with the current. They hid themselves in the branches, and, being over-looked by the Indians, finally reached the shore and returned to Hurtado with their tidings of disaster. The commander was so disheartened that he at once abandoned his post on the Rio Negro and hastened to Darien with all speed. It is surprising that Zemaco did not attack him when on the way, as he had an overwhelming force, and his recent victory had inspired him with confidence; but as it afterwards was ascertained, he was then in secret conference with the caciques of all the provinces, four in number, for the purpose of totally exterminating the Spaniards. Hurtado carried the tidings of this conspiracy to Darien, having received intimation of it from a captive; but the inhabitants considered his fears of an uprising largely imaginary, incited by his recent disaster, and made no preparations for receiving the enemy if he should appear.

At this time there comes into view once more the beautiful Cacica, who had been left in Darien when Balboa went on his expedition up the Atrato. She had urged him to take her with him, saying that her place was by her lord and master's side; but he had refused, because, as he said, space on board the brigantine was limited, and there was room for soldiers only. He had given his house into her charge at parting, and when he returned she proudly showed him what she had done to improve its condition, receiving his praises therefor with great delight. But rumors soon reached Balboa that during his absence the Cacica had received under her roof a young warrior, who had come and gone at night—as a spy might have done, said the sentinels who watched outside the walls of the town. These rumors were verified by reports from the spies whom Balboa himself had left to watch the Cacica while he was away. He ardently loved her—of that there could be no doubt; but, as a Spaniard, he was naturally suspicious.

These spies were certain that the visiting Indian was a warrior of Zemaco's band, and thought he might be a relative of the Cacica, or a former lover whom Balboa had supplanted. They, too, sought to intercept him; but the wary Indian escaped them every time, and they could only report that he had been there and undoubtedly held conference with the Cacica. When Balboa heard these reports he was deeply disturbed, for, notwithstanding his suspicions, he wished to have confidence in his mistress, and disliked to think evil of her. He was uncertain whether he had better keep the information to himself, and meanwhile watch the girl narrowly for signs of deceit, or openly accuse her of treachery to his trust. He adopted a middle course, and one day, while they were conversing upon the events of the expedition, artfully contrived to involve her in the confession that hardly a day had passed in which she had not indirectly heard from him.

"And who was the messenger, my love?" asked Balboa, calmly, but with his heart beating furiously and his eyes flashing.

"My brother, sometimes, my cousin, and again my brother—for, you know, I have many brothers," replied the Cacica, artlessly.

"Yes, I know," rejoined Balboa. "But why should they come to you so frequently, and always at night?"

"Because I wanted tidings of you, my lord; and for that they could not come too often! At night, too, because they could not get within the town by daytime. For there were sentinels and spies, my lord. Did you not know there were spies?" asked the Cacica, archly, her eyes dancing mischievously.

"I—I knew there were spies," answered Balboa, hesitatingly. Then, suddenly assuming a stern and wrathful expression, he grasped the girl's wrists and, looking straight into her eyes, demanded: "What did your people tell you when they came to my house in the night-time? Did they say aught of the cacique Zemaco and of the conspiracy he is forming against me? Tell me, and truly, girl, for if thou liest thou mayst lose thy life!"

"I will tell you," answered the Cacica, slowly. "Not because you threaten me, but for the love I bear you. My life is yours, to take at any time." She returned his gaze fearlessly, and in her eyes Balboa could detect no trace of deceit or alarm.

"I am a cacique's daughter," she continued, proudly, "though in your eyes a savage and a slave. Your life and the lives of your friends are in my hands—until I tell you; then my life and the lives of my people are at your mercy. Yet I will tell you, because you are still my lord, and I have left my people to go with you and stay within your house.

"Know, then, that my brothers came to warn me to fly with them and hide in the mountains, for the men of my race can no longer endure the atrocities committed by the invaders, and are resolved to fall upon them soon by sea and by land. In the town of Tichiri are collected one hundred canoes and five thousand warriors, and the preparations are made for striking a blow that shall destroy your power forever!"

IX

HOW THE CONSPIRACY WAS DEFEATED

1512

THE story told by the Cacica bore the stamp of truth, but Balboa was, or pretended to be, unconvinced, and induced her to send for the brother who had revealed the plot, that he might question him. As she hesitated, he said, "Since he desired you to go with him, you can say you are ready, and he will return."

"Yes, he will return. But how will he be received?" she asked, dubiously. "I would not have harm come to him, for his warning was from love of me, my lord."

"And for love of me I ask you to send for him," replied Balboa, evasively. He had released the Cacica's hands, and she had fallen into a hammock, where she lay listlessly, with a look of distress in her eyes and a great fear at her heart.

She could not understand how one she loved would willingly cause her pain; but she felt that Balboa was pressing home a weapon that might pierce her heart and end her days in misery. She had entangled herself in a net of her own weaving, however, and there was but one course to pursue. So she sent for the brother who, in his anxiety to save her from the massacre in which the Spaniards were about to be involved, had given the warning. He was one of Zemaco's warriors, and employed as a scout. Upon receiving a message from his sister he at once hastened to her side, whence he was torn by emissaries of Balboa, who cast him into a dungeon. There he was promptly visited by the magistrates of Darien, at the head of whom was Balboa, and severely questioned as to what he knew of the plot. He denied all knowledge of Zemaco's movements, and one of the magistrates cried out: "Then put him to the torture. Bring a bowstring hither!"

This order having been complied with by the jailer, he then said: "Bind it about his forehead, and twist it till his eyes begin to bulge! Perchance then he will tell what he knows."

This was done, and the cruel jailer twisted the bowstring with a stick until the Indian's eyes seemed about to burst from their sockets. Unable longer to endure the torture, he cried, in agony, "Oh, release me, and I will indeed tell all!" Then he fainted, for he was but a youth, and, though accounted as a warrior, was yet of slight physique and delicate. Vasco Nuñez de Balboa, who was standing by, could not but have noted his resemblance to the Cacica, whom he had often sworn he loved; yet he made no effort to release him.

The unhappy youth related what he had told his sister, and the story was the same that she had told, only there was something added. Gasping for breath, and with temples throbbing from agonizing pain, the hapless boy said that Zemaco had long before plotted the death of Balboa, and had for this purpose posted his warriors in disguise among the Indian laborers in the fields. They watched for weeks an opportunity to take the commander off his guard; but, though they valued not their lives at all, they were intimidated by the horse which he rode and the long lance he carried, and finally gave up the attempt upon his life. This failure had determined Zemaco to form the conspiracy with the other caciques, and to this scheme he was devoting all his energies."

As the boy proceeded with his relation, and detailed the means by which the plan against Balboa's life had been frustrated, it flashed upon that worthy that his going to the fields every day fully armed and mounted on horseback was owing to the Cacica's pleadings. Otherwise he would have gone without armor, in his doublet and hose, and on foot. Thus he would certainly have fallen a victim to the Indian's rage, and thus—it became evident even to his perverted sense—he owed his life to the sister of that frail boy before him, whom he had allowed to be tortured. Then his heart misgave him surely, and, awaking from the trance into which his evil thoughts had plunged him, he exclaimed: "Release that youth. Cast off his bonds and bathe his brow where the cord hath wounded it. He hath done nothing, and I did not mind to torture him to extremity; only to elicit the truth—and that we have done. So set him free."

The magistrates murmured and protested: "It is not customary, nor is it safe, to set free one who has been put to the torture, lest, in revenge, he hold murderous plans against us. Let us now finish him, with the sword or with the garrote, and done with it."

"Nay, nay!" exclaimed Balboa, excitedly. "I am governor, though you are, by my grace, the magistrates. I take this youth under my protection, and woe be to them who dare molest him!"

"As your excellency commands," retorted one of the magistrates. "He certainly hath claims upon you, if what rumor says may be believed: to wit, that his sister is thy—"

"That for thy insolence," exclaimed Balboa, stopping the objectionable word with a blow on the magistrate's mouth. "Let it be known that this youth hath my protection, and," he added, with an ominous frown, "let what may please you be said about it—behind my back; but not in front of me!" With that he strode out of the dungeon, leading the wondering Indian by the hand. And thus, bruised and disfigured, the trembling youth was taken to Balboa's house, and left there to be cared for by the Indian maiden.

It may seem to have been the refinement of cruelty thus to force upon the Cacica this victim of the Spaniards' barbarity; but in the eyes of Balboa she was merely a savage whose charms had ensnared him temporarily. Possessing neither delicacy nor keen moral perception, he mistakenly reasoned that the Cacica would overlook this wanton outrage upon her brother and forgive the perpetrators of it. She was his slave, subject to his every whim; but still she had a heart and a conscience, and she was capable of resentment. Though she had so carefully concealed her feelings that he imagined she would always be mild and passive, no matter what occurred, the Cacica really possessed a deep, revengeful nature.

When Balboa and her brother appeared before her, she clutched at her heart, as if to still its beatings, but said nothing, though a single glance told her what had occurred. She led her brother away, to a hut outside the palm-thatched structure which served Balboa as a dwelling, and was about to bathe his bruised forehead, when he repulsed her with a gesture of disgust.

She did not ask why, for she knew, and he did not waste words in telling her that she was a traitress, and was solely responsible for what had occurred to him. In silent dignity he gathered up his bow and arrows, which had been left with the Cacica when he was thrust into the dungeon, and without one word of farewell stalked off into the forest.

Then the Cacica knew that she had incurred the hatred of her tribe, as well as lost the respect of her master, by revealing the plot of Zemaco. She had done it for love of Balboa, as she had assured him; but now that she realized her position, as an outcast from her people, and, despised by the brother who had risked his life to save her own, she hated her master, and loathed him. Thenceforth she lived only for revenge; but, with the cunning of a savage, she concealed her real feelings from Balboa, and appeared to him only the dutiful slave. She lived silent and apart, but ever nursing a scheme of vengeance which in due time cost Vasco Nuñez de Balboa his life.

Through the treachery to her people of the Cacica, and the confession elicited by torture from her unhappy brother, Balboa came into possession of all the facts regarding the purposed insurrection of the caciques. He lost no time in acting upon this information, but promptly summoned his officers in council. His chief reliance was, as may have been divined already, the stout-hearted Colmenares, who had shared with him the dangers of several expeditions, in all of which he had borne himself with courage and resolution. While the magistrates were uncertain what course should be pursued, some advising an immediate retreat from a place so fraught with danger to themselves, both from the savages and from the climate, which was killing off the settlers by scores, Colmenares alone gave his commander the advice he liked. Balboa had settled in his own mind what he should do, but he desired to be supported by a certain show of authority, conferred by his coadjutors, in order to have a loop-hole for escape in case the adventure should prove disastrous.

"I can conceive of no other course than immediate pursuit," said the gallant Colmenares. "The redskins meditated taking us unawares and putting us to death, without a possible opportunity for escape. Hence they must have determined upon attacking us both by sea and by land. In sooth, the great gathering of canoes at the town of Tichiri shows that. What, then, is the proper mode of attack for us to adopt but their own, only in the reverse? That is, a body of our troops to proceed by water and another by land, thus taking the savages by flank and cutting off all chance of retreat. So far as our ability goes to combat them, you will of course agree with me that there is no great risk. And this I say with due regard for truth."

"Which I have always found thee to observe, and also to weigh carefully the things that make for success as well as defeat," replied Balboa. "In short, Rodrigo, thou'rt a careful commander, and thy scheme was the very one I myself should propose; but thou shalt have the credit of it. Take, then, Rodrigo, sixty of our men and embark them in canoes for Tichiri, while I, with seventy, will make a wide circuit by land, and thus we will fall upon the savages by front and by rear. Provision the boats for a few days only, for we shall in all probability find enough to eat by the way, and especially when we shall have taken the town and sacked it of what it contains. There are, I understand, five principal caciques in the league, four besides the arch-scoundrel Zemaco, and, assembling as they have been from every quarter far and near, they will have brought with them of supplies a sufficient store."

To the blare of trumpet and roll of drum, the entire garrison assembled within the stockade, and the two commanders picked their men from the ranks. Only the stoutest and most valiant were taken, those who had been tried before and were accustomed to Indian warfare; but nearly all desired to go, scenting spoils in prospective and tiring of inaction at Darien. Some could not, through being stretched on beds of pain, afflicted with wounds or disease; others could not, because of some disability of which their commander was cognizant; for he knew his little garrison to the last man, and was never at a loss to judge its strength or weakness. This was one secret of his success, another being his generosity; for he never withheld from any soldier his share of plunder, and was the last to think of himself.

"Oh ho," he laughed, as the volunteers came pressing forward, some shaking with ague, some limping on crutches, and all filled with enthusiasm. "So ye all desire to go? I' faith, but I wish ye all could do so. But go back to your posts, my good men, all that can manage a cross-bow or an arquebuse, and there keep vigilant watch, for who knows when, or in what manner, the foe may appear? Rodrigo and I will go forth, the one by water and the other by land; but there must perforce be a great gap of forest between us, through which the savages may come by stealth and fall upon the town. So, I say, keep watch by night and by day; and inasmuch as all are engaged in a common defence, and all entitled to equal shares in the spoils, even so shall it be."

Balboa was moved thus to deliver himself, because of ten thousand pieces of gold in the treasury, remaining undivided, which his enemies declared he intended to seize for himself and send as a donative to the king. For this reason he said, "We shall all share alike, from commander down to drummer-boy and trumpeter, and no man shall be deprived of his portion."

Then he marched off at the head of his armored band of braves, followed by the acclaim of those he left behind to guard the town. As for those who went with him: being all of them gallant souls, and generous to a fault, more disposed to fight for treasure than to quarrel over its division afterwards, they acquiesced without a murmur. Colmenares had already embarked his force of sixty men, when Balboa set off and lost himself in the forest with his seventy, so that the settlement appeared quite deserted.

The canoes of Colmenares were paddled by stalwart Indians taken from Careta's tribe, who were ignorant of the intended uprising, but could not, of course, be unaware that the expedition was proceeding against some of their people with hostile purpose. But they asked no questions, being reasonably certain that any such would be answered only by blows, and exerted their strength to such good purpose that by nightfall of the day in which they had embarked the Spaniards reached the vicinity of Tichiri. It was probably at or near a place now indicated on the map as "Punta Escondida," or Lost Point, and may have been thus named because of its vague and misty appearance in the shades of evening-time.

The shore seemed formless, and the forests that came down to the water stretched away black and forbidding, but the darkness was pierced by numerous points of light, where blazed the Indian camp-fires, and the "tam-tam-tam" of the drums proclaimed an assemblage for the purpose of war or conference. Colmenares waited till the drums had ceased their beating and the camp-fires had been swallowed up by the darkness, then the canoes were guided stealthily to the shore and the soldiers landed. The landing could not be made without some sound, such as the clanging of armor against armor, or the striking of sword or lance against a gunwale; yet the savages were so confident that no enemy was near that they were not disturbed, and slumbered while the force formed on the beach.

Preceded by the dogs of war, a pack of three having been brought by Colmenares for this very purpose, the Spaniards crept towards the camp, extending their line as they approached and perceived its great proportions. As the scent of the quarry reached their nostrils, the dogs could no longer be restrained, and leaped forward with deep-mouthed howls into the midst of the slumbering foe. Instantly arose shrieks of terror and pain as the beasts tore the inoffensive savages to pieces, and these were followed by wild tumult when the reports of arquebuses rose above all other sounds and the Spaniards burst from their concealment with loud shouts.

The terrified Indians knew not which way to turn, and huddled together in a mass, upon the outer skirts of which the hounds tore and ravened at will, while the cross-bows and musketry played destructively. Finally, perceiving that no opposition was offered, or likely to be, by the terror-stricken savages, Colmenares ordered the trumpeter to sound the recall, and the attendants to draw off the hounds; but it was a long time before the detestable beasts could be made to quit their prey.

X

DISSENSIONS IN THE COLONY

1512

THE savages surprised by Colmenares in Tichiri were under a captain, or sub-chief, whose name has not been preserved, but who received swift punishment at the hands of his own people for the crime of rebellion against Balboa. As soon as the Spanish commander had ascertained in which direction he was to look for the captain, he sent a small body of men in search of him. One of his own followers handed Colmenares the bow and spear that he usually carried, and, having presented this to the most sagacious of the hounds for his inspection, the brute sniffed the air an instant, then set off into the midst of the crowd. He and his two companions had been dragged from their victims while yet their blood-stained jaws held ghastly shreds and fragments of human flesh, and it was with his ferocious instincts roused to the highest pitch that the hound darted through the throng of Indians and leaped upon the cowering chieftain.

He was expecting death, and had calmly prepared himself to meet his fate; but such a terrible apparition as this he was unprepared for, and as the hound's fangs sank into his quivering flesh he shrieked in agony of pain and terror. It was with difficulty that the enraged animal was induced to release his hold, and suffered repeated blows from the mailed fists of his attendants before he would do so. Then the mangled savage was conducted before Colmenares, who had cleared a space in the centre of the camp and there held an impromptu court-martial upon the leaders of the insurrection. The instigator of the rebellion, Zemaco, had escaped, but four of the sub-caciques, including the captain of the band, were captured, owing to the swift and secret movements of the Spaniards.

With Colmenares acting in the capacity of judge, the proceedings of the "court" were confined to the identification of the victims as leaders and men of influence among the Indians. Their guilt was assumed from the positions they held, and as soon as their identity was established they were promptly sentenced: the captain to be shot to death with arrows by his own followers, and the caciques to be hanged. The sentence was carried out at break of dawn next morning. Scarcely had the sun gilded with his first rays the topmost branches of the forest trees, before the caciques were led out to meet their doom. A broad-based ceiba-tree, or silk-cotton, reared its huge bulk near the centre of the clearing, and up its buttressed trunk a pair of soldiers swarmed to its lower-most limb, over which they swung ropes made of grass, with nooses at their ends. These nooses were then slipped over the heads of the caciques, and soon they were suspended in the air, gasping their lives away, until they were naught but contorted corpses, upon which their former subjects gazed in speechless horror.

The extent to which the Indians had been terrorized by the Spaniards was more fully shown by what followed when the captain was brought to execution. He was placed with his back against the ceiba-tree, his arms and legs tightly pinioned, and compelled to face his slayers, who were archers selected from his body-guard. He faced them dauntlessly, and, calling upon the most skilful archer by name, directed him to shoot at his heart and end his misery without unnecessary delay.

"I blame ye not," he said to his men, "for ye are compelled, I know. Moreover, I shall the more gladly die, knowing that your weapons cause my death, and not those of the foe. Shoot straight, and trouble not thyself," he said to the foremost archer, who, as he was about to bend the bow, craved pardon for his act. The bowstring twanged, the chief's head drooped, and it was seen that the arrow had pierced his breast up to the feather. As the body fell forward several Indians sprang to catch it, and there was some confusion, during which it was perceived that the savage who had slain his chief was placing another arrow on the string. The quick eye of Colmenares caught him in the act, and fearing the shaft was intended for himself—as doubtless it was—he ordered him disarmed. One of the soldiers would have thrust him through with a lance, but the commander prevented him from doing this, perhaps realizing that he had committed atrocities enough, and had put upon this poor savage more than weak human nature could endure.

In the midst of the hubbub that ensued, there sounded the roll of a drum, followed by other noises, that proclaimed the approach of an armed force from the direction of the hills. In fact, Balboa and his men, who had been detained by the countless obstructions to a passage through a virgin forest, made their appearance shortly, and soon the two commanders met and embraced.

"Ha, Rodrigo," exclaimed Balboa, glancing at the grewsome objects hanging from the limb of the ceiba-tree, "but you have forestalled me, son, and saved me trouble. I had feared it might be necessary to swing up a savage or two, and it seems you have done it with despatch. Sorry am I that we were detained; but such is the fortune of those who seek to penetrate these forests. All the day and the night we have struggled against nature's impediments to our progress, and on my soul, Rodrigo, we are worn down and famishing."

"That I can well believe," answered Colmenares. "And we are not so fresh as we might be, nor have we had aught to eat since leaving the boats. But, if the camp-master has attended to his duty, there should be something, by this, awaiting us in shape of a breakfast. Let us seek him and see."

"A fine *cavalgada* [troop or herd] of captives you have, Rodrigo, and they should be sufficiently impressed by the punishment of their chiefs to behave well in the future."

"Doubtless they will," replied Colmenares, "for it was a conspiracy of the caciques, and not of the people at large. These are spirit-less wretches, most of them, and of themselves will be prone to keep the peace, I trow."

"Still, I think we will build a fort here in this wood, for it is a fine site for one, and the country at large is productive. Goldmines there are, too, back in the hills, and while old Zemaco is at large there will be no peace for us. Santa Maria! But I wish we could find that golden temple and its idol. Perchance we may, with a strong fortress here, and a garrison in command of a good man like thyself, Rodrigo."

Leaving Colmenares to erect a fortress on a commanding bluff overlooking the gulf, and eighty soldiers to hold the Indians in check, Balboa, with fifty of his own men, returned to Darien in the canoes. He arrived none too soon, as it chanced, for, taking advantage of his absence, some seditious fellows had stirred up a disturbance. He had left in command that Bartolomé Hurtado, who had been driven from Zemaco's country after the disastrous ending of the Dobaybe expedition. He was a favorite with the governor, but a man of no particular force (as may appear from his having fled the country he was left to defend), and against him rose the most unquiet spirits of the colony, led by one Alonzo Perez de la Rua.

Hurtado may have been arrogant when he found himself invested with sole authority in the settlement, and as Alonzo Perez was a cavalier of some distinction when in Spain, he took offence at the upstart's assumptions and refused to obey him. Not content with maligning Hurtado, he proceeded to declaim against Balboa himself, denouncing him as a man of low birth whom circumstance had invested with a brief authority, and who was, he said, a creature of their own creation. "A soldier of fortune," and "absconding debtor who ought to be cooling his heels in jail," were some of the milder things he said about the absent Balboa, who, as soon as he arrived and learned what had been done, promptly arrested Alonzo Perez and confined him in the calaboose.[2] As the testy cavalier had many friends in the colony, a party was quickly formed of considerable strength, which was opposed to Balboa, and for a time a collision seemed imminent between the rival forces.

Balboa had his soldiers at his back, and doubtless could have restrained the mutineers by resorting to force; but his penetrating mind looked beyond the present, with its temporary evils, to the future and its golden promises, so he released Alonzo Perez merely with a reprimand. This action for a time appeased the factious followers of Perez; but for a matter of hours only, and the next day they assembled anew. Taking advantage of Balboa's absence in the fields, whither he had gone to superintend the Indian laborers, they seized Hurtado, and possessed themselves of weapons, which they threatened to turn against the governor himself. Alonzo Perez was again in command, and being supported in his pretensions by a lawyer, one Bachelor Corral, he demanded that Balboa should at once deliver up for division among the colonists the ten thousand pieces of gold then in the treasury.

In the estimation of Vasco Nuñez de Balboa, this hoard of gold was of small account, as he expected and intended to add to it at least ten times that amount. Whatever happened, he was not willing to risk his life in defence of it, and learning that the mutineers intended to throw him into prison, provided they could secure his person, he hastily withdrew from the scene of strife, giving out that he was going hunting in the forest.

"Friend Hurtado," he said to his lieutenant, "I foresee that when those scoundrels get possession of that bone of contention, the ten thousand castellanos in our treasury, they will so abuse one another in the division of it that the sober-minded members of our community will be only too glad to recall me to restore order. Hence, let them have it. I had hoped to send it to our lord the king—and in truth I yet shall do so; but let them first have the fingering of it. Meanwhile, friend Bartholomew, we will go hunting, you and I, for it is better, methinks, to slay the beasts of the forest, which may aid in sustaining us, than our own countrymen—which we shall certainly have to do if we remain."

This was the purport of a conversation the shrewd Balboa held with Hurtado and his immediate followers, and his wisdom and foresight were soon clearly shown by the manner in which his scheme worked itself out. Alonzo Perez and his rabble seized the treasury, which he had left purposely unguarded, and with great hilarity proceeded to share among themselves the ten thousand pieces of gold. The result was what the crafty Balboa had foreseen, for a furious dispute broke out at once, and from words the mutineers came to blows.

There were still many adherents of Balboa in the community, but they had been awed into silence by the rabble. When the latter began quarrelling among themselves, however, and some of them even cried out, boldly, that their self-exiled governor had always been fair in the apportionment of the spoils, while Perez was extremely partial to himself, the friends of Balboa ventured to proclaim their own opinions.

"Who won this gold," they said, "but our own Vasco Nuñez by his enterprise and valor? Knowing him as we do, we say he would have shared it with the brave and deserving. [Probably meaning themselves.] But these men have seized upon it by unfair and factious means, and would squander it upon their minions. Out upon them, say we! Let us seize the ringleaders of this foul conspiracy and cast them into prison. Then we will send for our gallant governor and reinstate him in authority."

As most of the soldiers were absent with Balboa and Colmenares, and the mutineers were really in the minority, the temperate members of the community easily accomplished their purpose by seizing Perez, Corral, and other ringleaders and placing them in irons. They were confined in the fortress, where they had leisure to reflect upon their intemperate behavior, while a special committee of reputable citizens, appointed amid loud acclamations, was sent in search of the fugitive governor.

As may be supposed, they did not have great difficulty in finding him, for he had kept in touch with the proceedings through his scouts, and had not penetrated the forest so far that he could not be readily recalled. He was discovered in camp, surrounded by his faithful soldiers, and the whole company seemed in high spirits over their success in the chase. Wigwams had been built beneath the wide-spreading branches of umbrageous trees, and hammocks swung in which Balboa and Hurtado were lazily reclining—the time being in the heat of the day, when the delegates approached them with the proffer of reinstatement.

They had travelled fast and far, since early morning, and, having provided no refreshments for the journey, were faint, thirsty, and hungry. They looked longingly at the rude table made of palm-leaves spread upon the ground, and supplied with every kind of food and drink known to the colony. Indian cooks were busy at a barbecue over a camp-fire, the savory odors from which were simply maddening to the hungry delegates. They saw other Indians engaged in tapping the wild palms and ladling out calabashes full of palm-wine, while others still were preparing foaming chicha for their masters.

Now, the throat of the committee's spokesman was dry, and his tongue also, so that when he essayed to speak his voice entirely failed him, and he looked helplessly at his companions. Perceiving the condition of the delegates, Balboa, who had been watching them narrowly from the corner of his eye, hastily leaped from his hammock and exclaimed: "Not a word, Don Pedro, not a word, until you and your friends have slaked your thirst with draughts of our native wine. Cruel it was of me to keep you standing there, while this *desayúno* [breakfast] was being prepared, at which you must sit down, though it be so humble and poor of quality. Nay, I insist," he added, as the committee hesitated. "I know not your mission, *caballeros*; but, certes, you are faint and hungry, perchance thirsty also, so sit down, and answer not. Hither, mozos, with the calabashes of chicha and wine. Give my *compañeros* to drink, without delay."

The delegates gratefully accepted the food and drink so liberally profferred, and when they were refreshed the spokesman began his speech again: "Your excellency, we have come to ask you to return. The government goes ill without you—in truth, there is no government at all."

"Ha? But what of Don Alonzo and the Bachelor Corral?"

"They are in the caliboose, your excellency, and in irons."

"So? But how long will they remain, if I return. And what of the gold?"

"They will remain there at your excellency's pleasure; and the gold shall be collected and returned to the treasury."

"*Bueno*—good, very good. But how long, think ye, gentlemen, will ye continue in this chastened frame of mind? Not a month, not a week, before some low-born sons of Belial will provoke an outbreak against the authority of Vasco Nuñez de Balboa, and declare he hath no authority to govern. If I go, gentlemen, to Darien, then it must be under a pledge that ye all will unitedly stand by me, and sustain me in every effort for the public weal. What say ye?"

"We will, we will, your excellency. Only return!"

XI

BALBOA STRENGTHENS HIS ARM

1512

BALBOA stretched himself in his hammock, and looking at the delegates through half-closed eyes, as though he would resume his siesta, rejoined: "Gentlemen, I do not wish to return! But here is Don Bartolomé, who might be induced to act in my place. Let him go with you and assume the reins of government."

The delegates looked the confusion they felt, but said nothing, though Hurtado hastily exclaimed, "No, no; I care not to do so."

"Neither care I," said Balboa. "For what do I get by returning? Only the semblance of a shadow of authority. All the labors, all the insults attending the office; but never a *gracias, señor*—never a thank you, sir, get I. But here—ah, here I have my liberty. I ask no man whether I shall come or shall go. Here I can live free from restraint—I and my merry men. What say, compañeros, shall we return?"

"Never, no never!" came in a chorus from the soldiery.

"We are content here, are we not? The forest gives us sustenance—as ye see, gentlemen; it gives us shelter. Now that I am no longer compelled to hunt the red savage, and only the wild beast when I choose, rest and happiness have come to me."

The committee consulted together for the space of five or ten minutes, then the spokesman said, with a new note in his voice and a twinkle of triumph in his eyes: "Your excellency, we have a letter for you, which I herewith deliver. We know not what it contains, for, as you may witness, the seal is still unbroken; but from what tidings we have received from some high in authority at Hispaniola, we divine it refers to the great displeasure of his majesty, the king, as respects your doings at Darien. Here is the letter, your excellency."

Balboa took the letter without remark, and broke the seal. As he read, a serious expression came over his face, and he frowned severely, seeing which the delegates nudged one another and chuckled inwardly. He had good cause, in truth, to frown, for the letter was from his friend at court, Zamudio, whom he had sent to Spain to plead his cause. It informed him of the king's indignation, kindled by the charges against him lodged at court by the lawyer Enciso, by whom he was accused of being an intruder and usurper at Darien.

He was held responsible for all the disasters to the colony, and though in reality its founder, and pacificator of the savages, he was to be prosecuted on criminal charges, and might consider himself fortunate if he escaped with his life.

Such was the tenor of the letter, and such the purport of the information the committee had received before they left the settlement. This being so, it behooved Balboa to comport himself more in accordance with his changed position in the eyes of the committee, and after he had finished reading the letter he said: "This is an important communication, gentlemen, and to answer it properly I shall be compelled to return to Darien. If, then, it be your minds still to support me, we will soon set forth. But only on that understanding shall I go."

"We shall support you," answered the spokesman. "But let it be understood, however, that our support is given only as between you and other subjects of his majesty, the king. Should there be conflict of authority, as between you, Vasco Nuñez de Balboa, and his majesty, there will be no question which direction we should take."

"Nor would I, as a loyal subject of his majesty, ask more of you," rejoined Balboa, fervently. "Soldiers, companions, we will depart. Prepare for the march to town. Mozos, bring hither the wine and the chicha. Gentlemen, before we start let us drink to the health of his majesty. Long live the king!"

Then a wild scene ensued. Mingling promiscuously—cavaliers, soldiers of the ranks, and civic functionaries—the company all joined in drinking the health of their sovereign. They seized the brimming calabashes, and, lifting them to their lips, drank deeply to the toast, "Long live the king."

"Now fill again!" shouted one of the delegates. "Here's to the health of his majesty's most loyal subject, Vasco Nuñez de Balboa. May he live long as governor of Darien!"

"*Viva! viva!*" shouted the excited soldiery. "Long life to our governor!"

"And to his loyal supporters, these our friends," added Balboa, grimly smiling, and waving his right hand towards the delegates. "May they remain loyal—for the space of a week, and may they never have to choose between his majesty and myself, his most devoted subject and servant!"

The wine was soon gone, to the dregs, and with this as the parting toast the company broke camp and set out for town, where a new surprise awaited Balboa, in the arrival of two ships from Santo Domingo. They were laden with provisions and brought a reinforcement of two hundred soldiers and settlers, sent by the admiral, Don Diego Columbus. At the same time arrived, by the hands of the fleet's captain, a commission for Balboa as governor and captain-general. This had come from Miguel de Pasamonte, the royal treasurer of Hispaniola, a favorite of the king, sent out as a check upon the ambition of Don Diego, of whom his majesty was extremely jealous.

In this manner did fate seem to play at cross-purposes with Vasco Nuñez de Balboa, sending him tidings by one messenger of the king's disfavor, and by another of his esteem; though, to tell the truth, Pasamonte had assumed his majesty's approbation of his act, without right to do so. He had received from Balboa a large sum of gold, by a previous remittance, and this was the manner in which he requited the favor.

"Gold is most powerful, of a truth," whispered Balboa to himself, smiling the while, as he thought of the title it had won from Miguel de Pasamonte. "If, now, I could get to the king the ten thousand golden castellanos which I have recovered from those robbers, Perez and Corral, methinks such a donative might purchase exemption from the penalties which his majesty seems disposed to place upon me for my presumption in setting poor old Nicuesa adrift and sending Enciso back to Spain. Ha, I have it! I will myself go to court with the gold in my hand, and beard the royal lion in his den. Ten thousand pieces I have; at least ten thousand more may be raked and scraped in the colony, and, moreover, these shall be, to the king, but an earnest of much more to come."

Full of his new project, Balboa broached it to his counsellors without delay, but to his surprise they would not hear of it, neither would any person whatever in the colony. "No, no," they all exclaimed. "You shall not leave us, Vasco Nuñez. You are not alone our governor, but our guide and leader. You, only, are respected by the soldiers, feared by the savages, and we cannot do without you. Stay here with us you must; but we will send deputies to acquaint the king with the condition of the colony, to entreat the necessary military aid, and to plead your cause as though it were yourself in person, Vasco Nuñez."

They proved their sincerity by electing two deputies, one of them Juan de Caicedo, who had been inspector on the unfortunate Nicuesa expedition, and the other Rodrigo de Colmenares, "both men of weight, expert in negotiation, and held in general esteem." It was believed that they would satisfactorily execute their commission, and that both would return, since Caicedo left a wife behind him at Darien, and Colmenares had acquired much property, including a farm which he tilled with Indian labor, when not engaged in military operations. Balboa gladly relieved him from command of the fort at Tichiri, and rejoiced that he could send one who would so well represent his cause at court. By him he forwarded letters to the king, containing most extravagant accounts of the country's riches, not forgetting to mention the famed temple of Dobaybe, filled with gold, and the tales the

Indians told respecting the gathering of gold in nets. He showed this precious epistle to the colonists, and they were all so greatly impressed with it that, one and all, they contributed gold to the extent of their hoardings, which, added to the amount sent by the government to the king, represented a goodly sum.

Balboa's commissioners left Darien del Antigua about the end of October, 1512, and arrived in Spain, after a long and tempestuous voyage, in the early part of 1513. Had they been the only messengers from that isolated colony on the isthmus, all might have gone well with its governor; but, unfortunately for him, as we know, his enemies had preceded them and spread broadcast the most pernicious tales respecting the doings of the gallant adventurer, Vasco Nuñez de Balboa.

Leaving them for a time, while the ferment is working that eventuated in the downfall of Balboa, let us continue in his company until he has accomplished that great achievement due to his heroic efforts, and with which fame has inseparably linked his name—the discovery of the Pacific Ocean.

By the information conveyed through his friend at court, Zamudio, he was assured that lawyer Enciso had obtained a judgment against him in which he was condemned for costs and damages to a large amount. This was not all, for the king was very much incensed, and had issued a summons for him to repair to Spain without delay, there to stand trial on criminal charges respecting the outrageous treatment of Nicuesa, which had probably caused his death.

It will be admitted that Vasco Nuñez was then in a terrible predicament, and that there seemed no way out of it save by a desperate venture, by which he might perhaps retrieve his fortunes, win fame, and recover the lost favor of the king. Fortunately for him, the news conveyed by Zamudio's letter had been informal, and in advance of tidings direct from the throne, so there was still time for action. When the authoritative summons should come, it would be too late; hence he could not await the reinforcements so anxiously expected from Spain, and must accomplish whatever he did before their arrival. Thus the intrepid Balboa was thrown directly upon his own resources, and resolved to set forth without the assistance from his sovereign which he had every right to expect in an undertaking so vast and venturesome as his.

Desultory and apparently aimless as had been his doings hitherto, Balboa had never for a moment lost sight of that grand scheme he had formed for exploring beyond the mountains and revealing the existence, if possible, of the great "southern sea." Cacique Comogre's son had assured him that he would need at least a thousand men to assist him, and acting upon this sage advice he had waited for reinforcements before attempting the great adventure. But now, if he waited longer, he might forever lose the opportunity, for with the reinforcements from Spain would also come the order for his arrest and transportation, or at least his dismissal from office. What he did, then, must be done quickly as well as effectually, and he lost no time in perfecting his plans.

"While another and less intrepid spirit might have been overwhelmed by the prospects before him, Balboa was animated to new daring, and impelled to yet higher enterprises. Should he permit another to profit by his toils, to discover the great South Sea, and to ravish from him the wealth and glory which were almost within his grasp? No, a thousand times no! He had won the information at risk of his life; he would realize the profit of it, even at the risk of his life. At least, no other man should avail of it, to cheat him of his dues. He did, indeed, still want the thousand men who were necessary to the projected expedition; but his enterprise, his experience, and his constancy impelled him to undertake it, even without them. He would thus, by so signal a service, blot out the original crime of his primary usurpation, and if death should overtake him in the midst of his exertions, he would die laboring for the prosperity and glory of his native land, and freed from the persecutions which then threatened him."[3]

As he would be obliged to absent himself from the colony for a long period, he made every effort to weld the various elements into a civic body that should work harmoniously and resist the disintegrating forces from within as well as from without. His first step was to set free the ringleaders of the late insurrection, which done, and assured of their co-operation, he proceeded to select his soldiers. There was no lack of volunteers when it became noised about that Balboa was to set out on the grand expedition to which all the others had been in a sense merely preliminary, and he was at greater trouble to reject than to accept those who offered for the service. Desiring none but the most dauntless spirits, he put every man applying to the severest tests. In the first place, they must be capable of enduring fatigue and hunger; in the second, they must be unflinchingly courageous, for the route of march would lie through regions occupied by hostile Indians who were said to be cannibals and gave no quarter.

"My men," he said to them one day, when haranguing them for the last time, assembled on parade, "I shall not attempt to conceal from you the perils of this enterprise. In truth, they could not, in my opinion, be greater. And, while I shall always lead, as hitherto, asking no man to go where I would not venture in advance, yet you may not have the great incentive that moves me. So far as spoils and captives are concerned, ye shall share alike with me; but there is a greater motive than mere spoils. My ambition, as ye all have known for many months, is to achieve the discovery of that great ocean said to lie beyond the mountains. That is—that shall be—the object of my endeavors, and to that the getting of captives and the plundering of natives shall be subordinate. There will be, doubtless, vast spoil, for the country we are to enter has the reputation of being rich in gold and gems. There will be danger; there will be fatigues, deaths, wounds—but, above all, there will be glory—the *glory* of accomplishing something of which men have dreamed for many years, but have never achieved!"

"We will do it! The glory shall be ours!" shouted the men, vociferously. "Where you lead, Vasco Nuñez, we will go!"

They were probably as daring and reckless adventurers as had ever been gathered together since the New World was discovered, then twenty years agone, and that is saying much. There were, after Balboa had selected the most resolute and vigorous of the colony, one hundred and ninety in the band, all fighting-men of the most desperate type. They were armed with cross-bows and shields, swords, lances, and arquebuses, and there was no person in the company, not even the trumpeter or the drummer-boy, who had not been brought up in the profession of arms. Balboa looked them over proudly, and he also inspected their equipment carefully, for they were to accompany him, as he himself believed, not only on a most desperate venture, but on a veritable forlorn hope, which, if it failed, must end his campaigning, and perhaps his life.

The king must be placated and his favor recovered by no lesser gift than sovereignty over a sea which no man of his race had ever seen; and that was the impelling motive of Vasco Nuñez de Balboa in this marvellous enterprise.

XII

THE QUEST FOR THE AUSTRAL OCEAN

1513

A BRIGANTINE and nine large canoes carried the troops up the gulf to the shores of Chief Careta's territory, where the force was augmented by a thousand friendly Indians, who served as guides and carriers, on the march from the coast to the mountains. Finding his Indian father-in-law well disposed, and no signs of disaffection, the commander left here nearly half his men, to guard the vessels and keep open a way of retreat, should it be necessary, and with one hundred picked soldiers began his perilous journey through the wilderness.

He had left the settlement on September 1st, and on the 8th arrived at the frontier of Cacique Ponca's territory, but found his village abandoned and without a sign of life within its limits. Ponca, it will be remembered, was the inveterate enemy of Careta, and as he knew the latter was in league with Balboa, he had fled with all his people to the mountain fastnesses. He was extremely reluctant to emerge from his retreat, but was at last induced to do so by repeated offers of friendship, conveyed by the peaceful Indians, and when he finally came out was won by Balboa's kindness and induced to reveal to him all he knew.

It was not politic, the governor thought, to leave behind him one so powerful as Ponca inclined to be hostile, and, moreover, he alone could furnish guides to the sea that lay beyond the mountains. These he freely placed at Balboa's disposal, at the same time not only confirming the truth of the story told by Comogre's people, as to the existence of a great sea, or ocean, but adding that the country adjacent was rich in gold. In the excess of his friendship, he presented Balboa with some golden ornaments—receiving in exchange glass beads and other trifles, precious in the sight of the Indian—and furnished the army with provisions for the journey. The golden ornaments, Ponca assured Balboa, came from the country bordering upon the great sea, to gain a glimpse of which it would only be necessary to ascend a high peak rising above the cordilleras, and visible from the village they then occupied. This peak seemed to pierce the skies, to such an altitude it rose above the surrounding hills, and its broad shoulders were covered with dense forests, so that it appeared like an island in an emerald sea.

With the departure from Chief Ponca's country the real labors of the journey began, for there was no open trail through the mountain wilderness, white men never having been there before. The Spaniards were compelled to hew their way with sword and axe, scale rugged precipices, and ford the torrents of numerous rivers. Friendly Indians carried the provisions, and the heaviest pieces of armor, but even though lightly clad and burdened only with their weapons, many of the soldiers were overcome by the combined effects of fatigue and climate, so that in the end less than seventy remained with their commander, the others having fallen by the way. Such as had strength enough returned to Coyba; but there were some who, unable to endure the journey, sank to the ground and never rose again.

Steadily climbing, at the rate of two or three leagues a day, about September 20th the little band of soldiers reached a broad plateau covered with a tangled forest through which ran deep and rapid streams. This was the country of a warlike cacique named Quaraqua, who, discovering this small body of strangers invading his province, and never having had experience with Europeans, prepared to give them a warm reception. He was at war with Ponca, and that was enough to provoke his ire, so he took the field with a swarm of ferocious savages, and thought to frighten the Spaniards by a display of force. He and his warriors were armed with spears, bows and arrows, and two-handed battle-axes made of wood, but almost as hard and as heavy as iron. They thought themselves invincible, in their ignorance of warfare as conducted by the Christian, and, yelling furiously, poured upon the Spaniards like a mountain torrent.

Sturdy Balboa was leading the advance, as usual, with his inseparable companion Leoncito by his side. This battle-scarred veteran was a hound of scarce more than medium size, but as strong and fierce as a lion. He was not only leonine in his majestic bearing, but in color also, for his hue was tawny, like that of the king of beasts. As he was considered by the soldiers the equal of any member of the force, he drew pay as one of them, and during his various campaignings earned for his master upward of a thousand crowns. The Indians of the coast country knew him well by reputation, which was so terrible that merely the sight of him would put a thousand to rout. But these Indians of the mountains knew neither the dog nor his master—though to their sorrow they were soon to make their acquaintance.

At sight of the warriors emerging in serried masses from the forest depths, Leoncito growled ominously, and as they approached within bow-shot he sprang to meet them with long leaps. A shower of arrows was sent at him and he was struck by several; but his progress was not stayed until he met a warrior in the oncoming ranks, whom he seized by the throat and bore to the ground. A moment later the hapless savage was a mangled corpse, and his fate was shared by others in swift succession, as the furious beast tore his way through the barbarian phalanx, leaving terror and destruction in his wake. The savages were surprised and alarmed by the advent of this strange animal in their midst, but they were absolutely terror-stricken when the cross-bows and arquebuses sent forth their messengers of death. Many were slain as they stood petrified with astonishment and terror; for this was their first experience with fire-arms, and they could not conceive whence came the rolling thunder of the explosions and the sheeted lightning of the flames. After the first discharge came in ringing tones Balboa's battle-cry, "Santiago, and at them, compañeros!" With bright sword drawn and gleaming in the air, he sprang towards the foe, followed close by his men.

Then ensued a scene of carnage the like of which has been many times witnessed in the encounters between Spaniards and the Indians of America. It is not a pleasant scene to dwell upon, so let it suffice to state that this "aboriginal Regulus," the rash though gallant Quaraqua, together with six hundred of his warriors, lay dead upon the field after the charge was over. Some had been pinned to the earth with lances, some cut down by swords, and others torn to pieces by the blood-hounds.

Having thus removed the obstacles to their advance, the Spaniards entered Quaraqua's town, which they quickly spoiled of all the gold and other valuables it contained. This booty Balboa shared equitably among his followers, reserving for himself no more than any other got, after deducting one-fifth the total amount for the king of Spain. By his eminent fairness to the soldiers, and by his courageous bearing on every occasion, Balboa wins the admiration of all who become cognizant of his exploits; but alas! his escutcheon is stained with the blood of many innocents. Among the prisoners taken in the town were fifty or sixty male Indians, dressed in robes of white cotton after the manner of women, and these, their enemies said, were given to unnatural crimes and followers of the devil. Whether they were or not, the Spaniards did not pause to inquire, but let loose their blood-hounds, who tore them limb from limb.

The village which Balboa had won at such cost of blood and suffering was situated at the very foot of the mountain whence, the Indians told him, the great sea could be distinctly seen. He had brought woe and desolation to its homes, but by his harsh measures the Indians had been thoroughly cowed, and, after sending back the subjects of Chief Ponca, he selected guides and carriers from the surviving Quaraquanos. As his men were exhausted by the fatigue of fighting, and in need of all their energies for what was to come, he ordered them early to rest, after they had partaken of a bountiful supper supplied from the provisions found in the village. Some were disabled by their wounds, and these were to remain behind while he, with the strong and able-bodied, pushed on over the last stage of their eventful journey.

Having made every preparation for the morrow, after posting sentinels about the camp, Balboa retired to his hammock, but not to sleep. The events of the day had been so exciting that he lay awake all night, thinking, not of what had occurred, however: not of the lives he had taken, the crimes he had committed; but of what he was to see from that rock-ribbed mountain-peak, with its head in the stars above the sombre forest. It stood out black against the sky, provokingly near, yet aloof and isolate—this peak which he had sought for many months. It had stood there for uncounted centuries, and during the æon of its existence it had never been visited by civilized man. He, Balboa, would be the first to scale its sides and stand upon its summit, the first to gaze upon the view it might reveal.

Such thoughts as these kept Vasco Nuñez de Balboa awake while his soldiers slept. So absorbing were they that he hardly heard the groans of the wounded, the cries of anguish from the poor wretches on the battlefield. Wives, mothers, and children of the dead warriors were groping in the darkness for their loved ones, and when they found the objects of their search they rent the air with piteous lamentations.

At last the dawn dispelled the shades of night. Bounding from his bed in the ocean, the morning sun sent his rays athwart the vast expanse of forest and illumined the peak in the sky so that it shone like gold. It appeared to Balboa like a beacon-flame beckoning him onward, upward, and with feverish eagerness he spurred his men to activity. It had been his intention to start in the gray dawn, to avail of the morning coolness and freshness; but his soldiers were stiff and tired, and moved slowly, so that it was within two hours of noon when they emerged from the forest and saw the great peak standing stark before them.

DISCOVERY OF THE PACIFIC

"Stay ye here," said Balboa to his men, "while I ascend yon mountain-top." Leaving them huddled together at the dividing-line between the rank growth of the forest and the sparse vegetation of the higher altitude, he pushed onward alone. His heart beat high with expectation as he clambered over rocks that had been smoothed and polished by centuries of storm and finally reached the summit. There before him lay the view he had so long hoped to behold: a wilderness of forest, gemmed with sparkling streams, and bounded by the watery horizon. There lay the sea, or ocean, widely extending along the sky-line, vast, seemingly boundless, glittering like a diamond beneath the sun.

Thrilled by the sight, the conqueror stood for a moment spellbound, then sank upon his knees and, extending his arms seaward, gave thanks to the Almighty for the great privilege which had been vouchsafed him, as the first European to behold the southern sea. Rising to his feet, he waved his hands, and shouted to his men, "Come hither, and gaze upon that glorious ocean which we have so long and so much desired to see!" They flocked tumultuously over the rocky peak, and after them the Indians, who were extremely surprised at this outburst of joy and wonder over a spectacle with which they and their fathers had been familiar for many, many years.

After his excited companions had gathered around him, Balboa said: "Let us now give thanks to God, who hath granted us this great honor and privilege. For we behold before us, friends, the object of all our desires and the reward of all our labors. Before you roll the waves of the sea which was announced to us by Comogre's son, and which, no doubt, encloses the vast riches of which we have heard. We are the first to gaze upon it and shall be the first to reach its shores. To us belong their treasures, and ours alone shall be the glory of reducing these immense dominions to subjection in the name of our king, and of causing to be shed upon them the light of the only true religion. Follow me, then, faithful as hitherto, and, I promise you, the world shall not behold your equals in wealth and glory!"

The companions of Balboa, then reduced to a little company of sixty-seven, received his words with acclamation, and all embraced him, while the chaplain of the expedition, one Andres de Vara, chanted in solemn tones the beautiful anthem beginning: "*Te Deum laudamus*—Thee, O God, we thank." A great tree, which had been brought from the forest for the purpose, was shaped into a cross and raised on the spot whence Balboa first beheld the ocean. Around this was piled a mound of stones, to keep it in position, and then the company knelt in reverence before the holy symbol, while the chaplain offered renewed thanks for the inestimable privilege that had been accorded them.

Wrought upon by the sublimity of the scene, and filled with joy at the prospect of boundless wealth and conquest opened to them by the illimitable ocean spread out at their feet, the Spaniards rose to the dignity of the occasion, and showed themselves capable of elevated sentiment. Their leader had imbued them with his own enthusiasm, had invited them to share in the honors and glory of his great discovery, and they declared they would follow him to the shores of the great sea, and beyond. After signing a testimonial to the effect that they took possession of the sea and its shores in the name of the Castilian sovereign, which was duly attested by a notary, Balboa and his companions descended the sierras towards the south.

The date of this memorable discovery, as witnessed by the instrument the Spaniards signed, was September 25, 1513. They had been more than three weeks in accomplishing the journey from the north coast of the isthmus to the mountain-top, after fighting their way through difficulties and dangers which men of iron alone could have confronted and overcome.

Sometimes, says their chronicler, they had to penetrate through thick and entangled woods, sometimes to cross lakes, where some were lost in the depths; they had rugged hills and mountains to climb, precipices to scale, and deep and yawning gulfs to cross, upon frail and trembling hammock-bridges made of forest vines. From time to time they had to make their way through opposing bands of Indians, who, though easily conquered, were always to be dreaded, and upon whom they depended for their precarious supplies of provisions. Altogether, the toils, anxieties, and dangers of these Spaniards led by Balboa formed an aggregate sufficient to break down the strength and depress the mind of any, indeed, but "men of iron alone."

XIII

ON THE SHORES OF THE PACIFIC

1513

AMONG the *conquistadores* of America there is no more heroic figure than Vasco Nuñez de Balboa, who looms large in history, second only to Columbus, perhaps, in the magnitude of his discovery. The admiral himself had sought persistently for a passage into the ocean, which he firmly believed existed beyond the continent by which he was confronted in 1502; but it remained for Balboa to reveal that ocean seven years after the great navigator had passed away. Balboa is also the most picturesque figure in the conquest of America by the Spaniards, and especially when, at the culmination of his efforts, he stood with sword in hand, and armor-clad, "silent, upon a peak in Darien."[4]

He was then at the zenith of his power, as well as in possession of the health and strength of vigorous manhood, for he was but thirty-eight years of age at the time he made his great discovery. For a few months only he was to retain that power undisputed; then was to ensue a period of depression in his fortunes, followed by his early death. So long as he remained at a distance from Antigua del Darien, devoting himself to original research in the wilderness and the subjugation of the natives, his success was unparalleled; but whenever he returned to the settlement disaster seemed to welcome him.

Leading his enthusiastic soldiers down the southern slopes of the mountain, Balboa entered the province of a cacique named Chiapes, who, unaware of what had happened to his northern neighbor, Quaraqua, like him offered battle to the strangers. They were few in number, wayworn and hungry-looking, so he set upon them with his warriors—and his experience was like that of all others who had opposed Balboa, who poured a volley from his arquebuses into the ranks of the enemy, and then, in the confusion that followed, let loose the dogs of war.

Stunned by the reports of the guns, confused by smoke and flames, and overcome with astonishment, many of the Indians fell to the ground and became easy prey to the blood-hounds, while many others were made captive. To these latter the Quaraquano guides made such representations of the Spaniards' power to slay by means of thunder and lightning, and of their magnanimity to the vanquished, that Cacique Chiapes issued from his hiding-place and appeared before Balboa with gifts of wrought gold amounting to five hundred pounds in weight. In return he received the proffered friendship of the commander, and trifles like hawk-bells, beads, and looking-glasses, with which he was greatly pleased and contented.

Their friendship having been established on a secure basis, Balboa sent back his guides and carriers to Quaraqua with orders for all his soldiers there, who were able, to join him without delay. While he remained in the cacique's village, three scouting-parties of twelve men each were sent out to explore the country between the mountains and the southern coast. These several parties were commanded by Juan de Escary, Alonzo Martin, and Francisco Pizarro, the last-named—then a lieutenant or captain under Balboa—to become, in the wisdom of Providence, the conqueror of Peru. The scouting-party under Alonzo Martin was the first to reach the sea-side, and, finding on the beach an Indian canoe, the captain stepped into it and was pushed by his men out into the water, so that he could rightfully claim to be the first European to embark upon the southern ocean.

After his scouts had returned and the men from Quaraqua had rejoined him, Balboa himself set out for the coast, with less than thirty men, but all well armed, and accompanied by Cacique Chiapes and some warriors. They reached the sea-side on the last day of September, 1513, at evening, and as the tide was out sat down to await its return. The tides on the Caribbean coast of the isthmus rise and fall but little, while on the Pacific coast they are swift and turbulent. Soon the flats in front of Balboa were covered with foaming waters rushing in like war-horses, and, leaving his shady seat beneath the forest trees above the beach, he advanced to meet the curling waves. He was in complete armor, with a shining helmet on his head, breast-plate, greaves, and gauntlets. He must have seemed a brave and gallant figure indeed to Chiapes and his warriors as, drawing his sword and taking in his left hand a banner upon which was painted the arms of Castile and Aragon, he waded into the tide. The fierce waves assailed him violently, dashing first against his knees, then against waist and breast; but he withstood them valiantly, and, waving both banner and sword, shouted in a loud voice: "Long live the high and mighty sovereigns of Castile! Thus in their names do I take possession of these seas and regions; and if any other prince, whether Christian or infidel, pretends any right to them, I am ready and resolved to oppose him, and to assert the just claims of my sovereigns."

"Long live the sovereigns of Spain!" shouted the band on shore. "We will defend these their new possessions, even to the death, and against all the potentates of the world. *Viva! Viva!*" Returning to shore, Vasco Nuñez drew a dagger and with it carved a cross on the trunk of a tree, saying: "In this sign we shall conquer the heathen, and the blessings of our religion will we give them, in exchange for their barbarous practices. At the point of the sword will we compel them. Now taste ye the waters of this sea, and by its being salt shall ye know that they are of the ocean. They are salt, like the seas of the north; and the waters are vast, like the seas of the north; but from them they are separated by intervening mountains, as ye know, and can swear that they pertain to the great Sea of the South, which has been the object of long search, and at last is found and taken possession of for our dread sovereigns." Saying this, he caused the notary of the expedition, Andres de Valderrabano, to confirm all that had been done and said in writing, to which all present subscribed their names.

The spot where these historic incidents took place was a secluded nook in the great and tortuous bay of San Miguel, which deeply indents the southern coast of Darien, and lies southwest from the harbor of Careta, in a straight line about sixty miles distant. Both names still adorn modern maps of the isthmus, and indicate approximately the terminal points of Balboa's great journey from the north coast to the south, in the year 1513.

Cacique Chiapes and his men looked on in wonder while their new allies performed the strange ceremonials, remaining passive, but evidently not approving what they did not understand. When, however, a few days later, Balboa demanded of the cacique that he produce canoes in which he might embark for some distant islands, the latter protested that the time was bad for ventures on the sea. It was then the month of October, and that month, with November and December, comprised the season of storms, in which the winds were strong and variable, the seas at any moment liable to rise suddenly. But Balboa was persistent. He cared not for the storms. "My God will protect me," he said. "For am I not fighting the good fight and converting the infidels to the true faith? Go get the canoes."

Cacique Chiapes shook his head and said, "Perhaps your God may be stronger than my god; but no god that the Indians serve can protect us from the waves at this season of the year."

"That is because the god you worship is not the true God, whom we reverently serve," answered Balboa. "He hath protected us, 'mid dangers many, and will continue to do so."

But Chiapes was unconvinced, and as chief of an inland tribe, unacquainted with navigation, he hesitated to embark. He compromised, however, by guiding the Spaniards to the littoral province of one Cuquera, whose subjects were fishermen and owned a great number of canoes. Cuquera confirmed the statement of Chiapes, that the season was unpropitious for a venture at sea, but at sight of some pearls the chief displayed, which, he said, had been obtained on the islands off-shore, Balboa was more than ever determined to make the voyage. Overcoming the objections of the caciques, he crowded sixty of his men into nine canoes, and, accompanied by the faithful Chiapes, embarked upon the bosom of the gulf. Hardly, however, had the canoes reached open water, when they were assailed by a frightful tempest.

"Deafening was the tumult of the infuriated winds, which strewed the earth with the frail materials of the Indian huts. The rivers, swollen by the rains, overflowed their banks, tearing away in their violent course rocks and trees; and the tempestuous sea, roaring horribly among the rocky islands and reefs with which the gulf is filled, broke its waves against them, menacing with inevitable shipwreck those audacious mortals who had invaded this watery realm."

The intrepid spirit of Balboa had caused him to mock these dangers when on land; but soon he had good cause to repent his rash impulse, and, yielding to the importunities of the Indians, sought shelter on an islet. It appeared to be high and dry as the company landed there in the evening, but during the night the rising tide gained upon them until finally they were waist-deep in water. At or near midnight the wind went down with the tide, and at dawn next morning the unfortunate mariners sought their canoes, only to find them partially wrecked and all the provisions they had contained washed away. They spent part of the day in calking the open seams with grass and the bark of trees, and in the afternoon embarked in the crazy craft and sought the shore.

After hours of exposure to the tropic sun, they landed near nightfall at the upper end of the gulf, in the province of a cacique named Tumaco. The Spaniards, like the Indians, were weak and famishing, having labored all day without either food or drink; but no sooner had they made land in safety than the indomitable Balboa set out in search of the Indian town. It was at a little distance from the shore, and was not reached until midnight. The inhabitants had been informed of their coming and made a stout defence; but were soon routed by the Spaniards and driven into the forest at the point of the sword.

Groping within the bohios, or Indian huts, the victors found an abundant supply of provisions, with which they appeased their raging appetites, and also a large number of beautiful pearls, besides a quantity of gold. As some of the pearls were contained in shells freshly taken from the water, Balboa concluded that the seat of the pearl fishery was not far distant, and was very anxious to obtain possession of the cacique, believing that he could inform him in the matter. Having captured a son of Tumaco, he loaded him with gifts, such as a shirt made in Castile, and other trifles valued by the savages, and sent him in search of his father. The chief had sought refuge in a wild den among the rocks, deep in the forest; but he was very much impressed by the beautiful presents brought by his son, and consented to emerge from his retreat. When he appeared before Balboa he had with him six hundred pieces of gold, and pearls to the number of two hundred and forty. The gold was wrought into ornaments, and the pearls, though most of them large and perfect in shape, had been injured by fire, with which the Indians had opened the shells.

All this treasure Tumaco presented to Balboa, and when he saw with what joy it was received, and understood that the pearls were especially appreciated, he sent a party of his divers to search for more. Thirty naked Indians, accustomed all their lives to dive for pearls, went down the coast in a canoe, accompanied by six Spaniards as witnesses; but the sea was so rough that they dared not fish in deep water, where the large pearl-oysters lay. The storm, however, had caused a great number of oysters to be washed ashore, and there they collected more than ninety ounces of small though perfect pearls, which were freely given to the Spaniards. The best of these, with specimens of the oysters from which they were taken, were set apart by the conscientious Balboa, as an acceptable gift to his sovereign.

More precious than pearls, however highly they were valued by the explorer, was certain information conveyed to Balboa by Tumaco, confirming the rumors that had reached him in the interior, respecting a vast country to the southward, which abounded in gold and gems. This was Peru, subsequently to be subjugated by Francisco Pizarro, then a humble follower of Balboa, and with him on this occasion. In order to impress the Spaniards with the high state of that country's civilization, Tumaco described as well as he could the beasts of burden used by the inhabitants of the distant empire. He moulded in clay, it is said, a figure of the animal known as the *llama*, which the Spaniards, as they had never seen or heard of it before, supposed might be a deer or a tapir—the latter being the largest animal they had found in South America.

But, great and glowing as were Balboa's hopes respecting that wonderful country to the southward, he was obliged to confess himself unable to explore it at that season and with the small force at his command. He made an experimental voyage along the coast for several leagues, cautiously feeling his way through an inundated forest on the border of the gulf, but dared not venture out at sea, where the wild winds roared and the waves beat incessantly upon the shores of distant islands. Pointing to one of these islands about five or six leagues distant, Tumaco told Balboa that its waters produced the largest and finest of pearls, such as the Spaniards had never seen, for size and beauty; but he could not take him to it then, much as he desired to please him. The two chiefs, the Indian and the Spaniard, were then in the former's war-canoe, hewn from the trunk of an immense forest tree, and paddled by a crew of sixty Indians. The paddlers themselves were stark naked, but the heads of the oars they used were inlaid with pearls. Of this circumstance, says a contemporary chronicler, "Balboa caused a record to be made by the notary, for the sake, no doubt, of establishing the credit of what he himself should write to the sovereign (no less needy and covetous than the discoverers themselves) concerning the opulence of the new country."

Several weeks were consumed by Balboa in exploring the country adjacent to San Miguel, and on a day in the first week of November, Tumaco took him and his companions in his war-canoe to the uppermost end of the great bay. With them also was the still faithful Chiapes, who considered himself in some sort as Balboa's sponsor, and who, when the time for parting came, is said to have shed tears, so deeply was he affected. He gladly assumed the care of the Spanish sick and wounded, and took them with him to his village in the mountains, while Balboa, with his able-bodied veterans, essayed to return by another route across the isthmus. The territory at the head of the bay was controlled by Cacique Techoan, who vied with the other chiefs in bestowing gold and pearls upon the Spaniards, and who furnished them with burden-bearers and provisions for the journey.

That Techoan was not entirely disinterested was shown conclusively by his guiding them to the abode of a cacique whom he represented as a rich and powerful lord, but an insufferable tyrant. This tyrant was known as the "Crœsus of the mountains" (or its equivalent in the Indian language), and, as may be believed by those acquainted with the character of Balboa, the latter was not unwilling to seek him out and make his acquaintance. But Ponca (for that was his name) was not anxious to meet the Spaniards, especially when he learned that they were coming in company with his deadly enemy, and fled farther into the mountains, taking with him, it was thought, the bulk of his treasure. He left behind, however, some three thousand pieces of gold, which the Indian allies discovered and took to Balboa, who used every exertion to entrap him and force him to disclose the hiding-place of his vast wealth. He caught him at last; but when questioned as to his gold, Ponca answered that all he had the Spaniards already possessed, and that it had been left him by his ancestors. More than this he would not disclose, even when the cruel Spaniards put him to the torture, and, provoked by his obstinacy, in the heat of their passion, gave him and three companions to the dogs, who finished the revolting business by tearing them to pieces.

In extenuation of their cruelty the Spaniards afterwards described Ponca as a monster of depravity, with deformed limbs, a frightful countenance, and a sanguinary nature. The guilt of his death, said one of their countrymen, "rests more with the Indians than the Castilians; yet *they* were not the judges of Ponca!" They assumed, however, that any Indian who refused to reveal the hiding-place of treasures which they desired to possess was deserving of death, believing, as they did, that there was nothing of greater worth in the world than gold, or its equivalent in material wealth. Thus cheaply did they hold the lives of the Indians, reckoning their immortal souls as of less worth than perishable gold. In this respect Balboa was no better than his comrades, and in truth set them an example which they were not slow in following.

The senseless avarice of the Spaniards wrought its own retribution on this journey, for they had laden their carriers with gold to a greater extent than with provisions, and this was done notwithstanding their route lay through a sterile wilderness yielding no supplies. The consequence was that they soon began to feel the effects of famine, some of them, as well as many Indian carriers, sinking by the wayside to rise no more. Rumors preceding the Spaniards informed the natives that they desired, above all other things, gold and like treasure, and thus gold was invariably brought as a peace offering, to the neglect of provisions, so that the soldiers (says the historian who perused Balboa's journal) "yet wanted nourishment and pursued their melancholy way, cursing the riches which burdened but could not feed them."

Still they clung desperately to those riches, stained as they were with the blood of innocent Indians, and when Balboa learned that a short distance off the main route he was pursuing there lived a powerful cacique named Tubanamá, who had, according to report, vast stores of gold, he made a forced march and by a night attack fell upon and surprised him, with all his family. When threatened that unless he gave up his gold he should be tortured and thrown to the dogs, or bound hand and foot and cast into the river, he approached Balboa and, pointing to his naked sword, exclaimed: "Who that hath not lost his senses would think of prevailing against that weapon, which can cleave a man at a stroke? Who would not rather caress than oppose such men as thou? Kill me not, I implore thee, and I will bring thee all the gold I possess, and as much more as can be procured!"

XIV

A RIVAL IN THE FIELD

1514

CACIQUE Tubanamá was warlike as well as wealthy, but he had been completely cowed by Balboa's display of force and weapons, so that he readily complied with the Spaniard's demands. Sending his men into the forest, he remained as a hostage with his captor, while they ransacked his storehouses for gold. So successful were they that within three days gold was brought in to the amount of six thousand crowns; but even then Balboa professed himself dissatisfied and declared there must be much more concealed in the province. As Tubanamá positively declared to the contrary, he finally gave the cacique his freedom, but when he departed for the coast took with him, it is said, his eighty wives and eldest son.

Great quantities of virgin gold having been discovered in the mountain streams, he resolved to return, and found a settlement in that region, but the condition of his command at that time forced him to resume his homeward march without delay. Most of his men were now so exhausted that, like Balboa himself, who was ill of a fever, they had to be borne in hammocks on the Indians' shoulders. In this manner marching, and in such sorry state that by a concerted effort the caciques might have destroyed them utterly, the Spaniards approached the province of Comogre, where they found themselves among friends and on familiar ground. The old chief was dead, they were told, but in his place ruled the young cacique who had first informed Balboa of the South Sea and Peru. He received him hospitably, as before, and made him a present of all the gold he and his subjects had collected since they parted, in return for which Balboa gave him a shirt and a soldier's cloak. As he had embraced Christianity, young Comogre considered himself vastly superior to the pagans about him, and when clad in the garments of the Christians, he assumed the airs of a king and compelled his naked subjects to do him homage.

At this, or a point previously reached on their journey, the Spaniards were rejoined by the wounded and invalids who had been left with Chiapes. Though but a handful of soldiers, they had travelled in safety through the forests and defiles of the mountains, such was the terror with which the deeds of Balboa had inspired the natives. One of the provinces they had passed through was governed by a minor cacique named Bonouvama, who not only detained, but entertained them most hospitably with everything his territory afforded. When they left his town he placed himself at their head, and on arriving in the presence of Balboa, said to him: "Lo, we are here! Receive, O valiant man, thy companions safe and uninjured, even as when they entered my bohio. May He who gives us the fruits of the earth, and who creates the thunder and the lightning, preserve thee and them, my lord!"

Balboa was deeply affected by the cacique's speech and meritorious actions. He graciously replied that they should arrange a perpetual friendship and alliance, as he hoped to do with all the caciques of Darien, and after bestowing upon him some beads, toys, and a Spanish shirt, sent him back to his province greatly rejoicing. Although, as we have too often seen, he acted with great cruelty towards some of the caciques, to those who approached him in a pacific spirit he was ever friendly and benign. That he grew to understand the nature of the Indians is shown by his success in converting them from enemies to friends, and by the alliances which he cemented with more than a score of native caciques in the course of his wonderful journey. There never was a Spaniard among his contemporaries, excepting perhaps De Soto, who had such success with the aborigines. Columbus and Cortés, Pizarro and Velasquez (who conquered Cuba), and all others who came in their train, lamentably failed in their dealings with the Indians. Balboa's success with his men was no less than with the Indians he encountered, for he had a faculty for winning their affections and holding them, which no other commander of his time displayed. Pizarro approached him in this respect; but Pizarro received his initial training under Balboa himself.

Bidding Comogre farewell, Balboa led his men through the province belonging to Ponca, where he was met by four Castilians, who informed him that a ship and a caravel well laden with supplies had arrived at Darien during his absence, and that he was awaited there with great anxiety. Hastening thence to Coyba, the territory of his father-in-law, he embarked at the port of Careta for Antigua del Darien, where he arrived the following day, which was January 19, 1514, after an absence of four months and twenty days. Every week, nearly every day, that had passed since his departure had been filled with exciting incident, and, moreover, he had returned to report to his fellow-citizens of Antigua one of the greatest discoveries of the age. No wonder, then, that the entire population sallied forth to greet him at the gates of the town, and that they rent the air with shouts of joy and welcome.

Lamentations were mingled with the acclamations, for some who had gone out with him had found, instead of gold, only a grave in the forest. Some who returned were suffering from fevers and wounds received in conflicts with the Indians; but notwithstanding, it was declared that the expedition of Balboa to the shores of the great Southern Sea was the most successful of any that had ever been made in America. And when the plunder was displayed: gold by the thousand pieces, pearls by the hundred, brought in by scores and scores of captives who would serve in the future as slaves, the transports of the people knew no bounds. He was hailed as "Conqueror of the Mountains, Pacificator of the Isthmus, and Discoverer of the Austral Sea." Bringing with him more than forty thousand ounces of gold, innumerable cotton robes, and eight hundred Indians of service—possessor, in short, of all the secrets of the land, and full of auspicious hopes for the future—he was considered by the colonists of Darien as a being privileged by Heaven and fortune. Congratulating themselves on possessing such a chief, the Antiguans conceived themselves invincible and happy under his guidance and government.

"They compared the constant prosperity the colony had enjoyed, the splendid prospects before them, the certainty of success attending his expeditions, with the unfortunate enterprises of Ojeda, of Nicuesa, and even of Columbus, who could never gain a firm footing on the American continent; and this glory was yet enhanced when the virtues and talents of him who had obtained it were taken into consideration.... Among all these eulogiums none were so hearty as those which were given to his care and affection for his companions. Affecting no military discipline, but behaving more like their equal than their chief, he visited the sick and wounded individually, and condoled with them as a brother; when any one sank on the road from fatigue, he was himself, instead of deserting, the first to raise and encourage him. He would often go out with his cross-bow in search of game to appease the hunger of those who were unable to seek food for themselves; he himself would carry it to them, and by this care and kindness he so gained their hearts that they would follow him willingly whithersoever he chose. The remembrance of these excellent qualities survived for many years; and the historian Oviedo, who cannot be charged with lavishing his praises on the conquerors of Terra Firma, wrote, in 1548, that in conciliating the love of the soldier, no captain of the Indies had hitherto done better than, if any had done so well as, Vasco Nuñez de Balboa in Darien."

The rich spoils, including the forty thousand ounces of gold and the pearls, were fairly divided between the soldiers and the settlers, as the latter had held possession of Antigua as a base of supplies and operations while the former were actively engaged in the field, and had thus contributed their share towards the success of the expedition. The "king's fifth" was religiously set apart, in the first place, and soon an opportunity offered for sending it to Spain, in charge of a soldier who had accompanied him when the South Sea was discovered, Pedro de Arbolancha. As he was an intimate friend of Balboa, who had proven himself a trusty companion in the midst of great vicissitudes he was despatched as an envoy to the court, not only with letters to the king containing a full account of the great discovery, but in charge of the sovereign's fifth and a donative of the largest and most precious pearls.

If he could have set out immediately after the return of the expedition, all might have gone well with Balboa's schemes of conquest and government; but his ship was delayed until the first part of March, and in the meanwhile events were shaping in Spain which imperilled not only the fortunes, but the life of the great leader. Balboa's former messengers, Caicedo and Colmenares, had arrived in Spain during his absence from Antigua, bearing to the king the tidings communicated by the cacique Comogre, and a request for reinforcements to the extent of a thousand men. Their testimony as to Balboa's unswerving loyalty to the crown, and the vast significance of the intelligence they brought respecting the existence of an ocean beyond the mountains, turned the tide of sentiment at court in his favor, and excited the swelling ambition of King Ferdinand. The sovereign had already listened favorably to the complaints of Enciso and other enemies of Balboa, and had issued an order for his arrest, even going to the extent of threatening to imprison his friend Zamudio on account of the zeal he displayed in his defence. But the more recent information placed him in a new light. The enormity of his offence was lessened by the great service he had rendered the crown. He was no longer regarded as a fugitive from justice, an absconding debtor, who had seized the government of Darien by force and caused the death of its real proprietor Nicuesa. He had made for himself a new name, and around his head already shone the halo of the great discoverer.

But again, the sovereign was involved in a complication which arose from the conflicting accounts from Darien. That there was dissension there, that the colony was threatened with extinction through the quarrels of unscrupulous men, he was well assured. The leader of those men, he had also been assured, was none other than Vasco Nuñez de Balboa. Accompanying the reports of dissension in the colony had come, as well, most convincing proofs of its prospective value to the crown in the richness of its resources. "And as the adventurers who went to America dreamed of nothing but gold—as gold was the object of their pursuit—as it was gold which they took forcibly from the Indians—and gold alone by which the latter purchased their friendship—gold which resounded in their letters and despatches to court—and gold which at court was become the sole subject of conversation and desire—the Darien, which appeared so rich in this coveted metal, lost its first name of New Andalusia, and was commonly called, and even named in the despatches, the 'Golden Castile.'"

Though it was mainly owing to Balboa's efforts that the isthmus won its new appellation, Golden Castile, and though he had in a measure retrieved himself, yet the king was unwilling to intrust him with its government. Casting about for some one to represent the crown with dignity and credit, he selected a cavalier who had served with distinction in the wars against the Moors, Don Pedro Arias de Avila, more commonly known as Pedrarias. He was an elderly man, who had won a reputation in his youth as a jouster in the tournaments, and who, beneath a chivalrous and courtly demeanor, concealed a nature narrow, mean, and warped by prejudice. He had certainly no qualifications for the office of governor; but he possessed the patronage of the powerful Bishop Fonseca, who then ruled the colonial affairs of Spain, and that sufficed to land him in the executive chair at Darien.

He sailed from Spain about the middle of April, 1514, and entering the Gulf of Urabá the last of June, cast anchor before the town of Antigua del Darien. His fleet was composed of five large vessels, and contained a gallant company, with everything needed for conquest and colonization. Balboa had asked the king for only a thousand soldiers, but Pedrarias sailed with a company of two thousand, some of them cavaliers of distinction, many wealthy hidalgos, and all well provided with arms, equipment, and money. They had heard the exaggerated reports from Darien, of gold that was caught in nets, which might be obtained almost without effort from the waters of every mountain stream, and were eager to join the fortunate adventurers under Balboa.

The king himself thought so well of the venture that he had expended upon the armada more than fifty thousand ducats, and had sent out with Pedrarias a number of friars, over whom was placed his favorite preacher Juan de Quevedo. He was consecrated as bishop of Antigua del Darien, which was elevated to the dignity of a metropolitan city, as capital of the Golden Castile. While the sovereign provided for the spiritual interests of the colony in this manner, at the same time he ordained that no lawyers should be permitted to practise there, as experience had shown they were detrimental to the welfare of new settlements. In spite of this inhibition, however, one lawyer went out to Darien as alcalde mayor, or chief judge, where he fully justified the king's apprehensions regarding men of his profession. His name was Gaspar de Espinosa, and though he knew little of the law, he knew enough to make a deal of mischief in the colony, and eventually became a tool in the hands of Pedrarias, by which he effected the downfall of his enemies, among whom he soon reckoned Vasco Nuñez de Balboa.

The fleet swarmed with cavaliers and men of distinction, but there was only one lady of importance aboard the flag-ship, the wife of Governor Pedrarias, Doña Isabel de Bobadilla, a distant relative of royalty and formerly a favorite at Queen Isabella's court. So attached was she to the crusty old cavalier, her husband, that, notwithstanding she was mother of several children, she chose to abandon them all and accompany the governor to his capital in the wilderness. Needless to say, she was a lady of grace and refinement, and deserved better of fate than to be wedded to a sanguinary monster such as Pedrarias soon proved himself to be. She has left no record of her sorrows;

but they must have been great, since the crimes she was compelled to witness were frequent, and revolting even to the hardened soldiery of Darien.

XV

PEDRARIAS, THE SCOURGE OF DARIEN

1515

AT the time of the fleet's arrival at Darien, the town of Antigua consisted of about two hundred huts thatched with straw, with five hundred white men and fifteen hundred Indians composing its population. It was badly situated, in a deep valley between high hills which cut off the salutary sea-breeze, but the soil was rich, and, owing to the exertions and example of Balboa, gardens of fruits and vegetables were already numerous and well tilled.

Since his return from the sea beyond the mountains, Balboa had devoted himself assiduously to the improvement of the colony: erecting huts for dwellings, extending the area of cultivated ground, and devising means for inspiriting the lonely inhabitants of this isolated post in the wilderness. The demands upon his time were constant and pressing, for he was looked up to as the savior of the colony, while the simple natives regarded him almost as a father, and came to him for advice on all occasions. Having heard nothing from Spain since the sailing of Arbolancha, the arrival of Pedrarias and his fleet took him by surprise; but it did not destroy his balance. If he had but known that, at that very time, his messenger was being received at court, and that the old king, charmed by the story of discovery, the pearls and the gold, already repented of the slight he had put upon him, Balboa might have assembled his veterans and prevented the landing of Pedrarias. They were only one-fourth the number of the new arrivals, but every man was a seasoned soldier, and there would have been little doubt as to the result of an encounter.

But fate played Vasco Nuñez false again, for Arbolancha had passed Pedrarias on the ocean and arrived in Spain too late to change the decision of the king, who then regretted that he had not rewarded Balboa with the governorship of Darien. He was the governor, in fact, elected to office by the votes of his adoring comrades; but Pedrarias came with royal authority, and Balboa bowed to the decree of the king.

There was doubt in the mind of Pedrarias as to the nature of his reception by Balboa; for he knew himself as a usurper, who had come out to reap the rewards of another, so he sent an envoy to announce his arrival and ascertain the sentiment ashore. This emissary, says the old chroniclers, expected to find the governor of the Golden Castile seated, of course, on a golden throne and lording it over a horde of captive slaves. What, then, was his astonishment to find the redoubtable Vasco Nuñez de Balboa, Conqueror of the Mountains, and Pacificator of the Indians, overseeing a group of natives who were engaged in thatching his humble hut with straw! He wore no robe of state, but merely a cotton shirt over one of linen, cotton *pantolones*, or wide trousers, and hempen sandals, called *alpargatas*, on his feet.

He looked up from his work as the messenger approached, and, seeing that he was a stranger, saluted him with courtly dignity. Without manifesting emotion of any sort, he received the message, to which he replied: "Convey to Don Pedrarias de Avila my congratulations on his safe arrival, of which I am rejoiced to hear, and say also that I am ready, with my companions, to receive and to serve him who cometh in the name of the king."

The news soon spread that a new governor had arrived, and, hastily arming themselves, some of Balboa's comrades began to assemble around their chieftain, imploring him not to allow his authority to be usurped, even by an emissary from the king. Their leader seemed absorbed in his work, to which he had returned after the departure of the envoy; but his thoughts were busy over the problem with which he was so suddenly confronted. Though outwardly calm, he was deeply disturbed by the action of the sovereign he had so loyally served, upon whom he had thrust inestimable blessings—who thus requited all he had done with insult and rebuke. But finally, in answer to the clamors of his friends, he slowly said: "Nay, nay, my comrades. Though doubtless we are strong enough to repel Pedrarias and his carpet knights, who come to harvest with their swords the crops we have planted with ours, and watered with our blood, yet will we not oppose him, for he comes with authority from our sovereign. And, I understand, there is with him fair Mistress Bobadilla, erstwhile a companion of our late queen, who is now with God in glory. So it behooves us, caballeros, to receive them gallantly, as if, indeed, we were glad to do so, and to place at their disposal the best we have—which, God knows, is poor enough."

Thus saying, Balboa strode within his house, and when he emerged again he had on his complete suit of armor; but his good sword was in its scabbard, and in his hand only the wand of office. Likewise unarmed were his battle-scarred followers, though clad in armor which was no longer bright and shining, but rusty, dented, and battered by blows from many a weapon wielded by arm of savage foe. These veterans suffered in appearance by contrast with the foppish cavaliers who landed from the fleet, nearly two thousand in number, brave in their glistening armor and confident from their numerical superiority. When they saw them, however, they smiled significantly, being well assured that they could defeat them in open encounter, and by no means afraid to essay it.

"They are our guests and our brothers, remember," remarked Balboa, as the veterans seemed disposed to murmur at his lack of precaution. "They come as we once came, hopeful, and expectant of wealth. Think, then, of the disappointment in store for them, and not of their arrogance. And, too, forget not the governor's lady. Ah, here they come! We must be at the boats to greet them, comrades. Into line! March!" The bugle sounded, the drum beat, and the veterans went to meet Pedrarias at the shore.

As the boat touched ground a plank was thrown out and across it walked Pedrarias, followed by his wife, the bishop, and the alcalde, behind them a train of cavaliers who formed a body-guard and led the way to the town, preceded by the veterans of Darien. Balboa doffed his helmet, and extended a hand to assist Doña Isabel ashore, as he said: "Thy servants greet and welcome thee, lady. To serve thee we are here; but we regret we have so little to offer one who deserves so much." And to the governor: "Don Pedrarias de Avila, thou art welcome, coming in the king's name, whose hand I kiss, whose orders I shall ever obey."

Doña Isabel was a tall and stately woman, scarcely past her prime, and still retaining some of the beauty for which she was famous when at Isabella's court. She was not insensible to the gallant bearing of the handsome cavalier Balboa, whose straight and stalwart frame was in decided contrast to her husband's misshapen body, and his frank countenance grateful to her gaze, after long acquaintance with the sinister face of Pedrarias. That she smiled graciously on Balboa at the end of his speech, and perhaps showed pleasure at his flattery, was not to be wondered at; but old Pedrarias noted these things with a twinge of ignoble jealousy, and frowned at his host instead of smiling.

"Where is the palace?" he growled at Balboa, as they approached his straw-thatched hut and halted at the door. "This is not a fit habitation for my wife to dwell in, let alone a domicile for the executive."

"That I freely grant, your excellency, and it vexes me that it be so," replied his host, with a smile and deprecatory wave of the hand. "But such as it is, I trust you and your noble lady will accept and avail of it, until we can erect a better, which we will do without delay."

They entered without another word, and seating themselves at the table, which Balboa caused to be spread with as great a variety as the settlement afforded, gazed at the meagre banquet with amused disgust. For, though there was an abundance of food, it consisted entirely of vegetarian products, such as maize and cassava bread, wild roots and fruits; and as for drink, there was no beverage except water from the river.

The frown upon the governor's face deepened to a scowl, but his wife broke into a merry laugh, in which she was joined by the bishop, who said: "So,

Señor Caballero, this is the best you can afford in this so-called land of plenty? Faith, I had heard we were but to open our mouths and luscious fruits would fall into them; while as for gold, we could kick it up in the streets, as it were."

Balboa was presiding at the table with a gracious dignity that, in the eyes of Doña Isabel, made ample amends for the lack of provand. An amused smile crept over his face, but he answered, gravely: "Needs it be said, your lordship, that this is the *best* we can afford? Would that it were not, for the sake of such distinguished guests as this day I am honored with; but, the truth to tell, we have not been compelled to fast on Fridays, merely, for meats of any sort have been hardly to be found. As for gold—well, my last remittance to the king was no less than fifty thousand ounces; but we did not by any means find it easy of acquisition, let me assure you. It is to be found far in the forest only, and must be won chiefly by toil, the sword, and the shedding of blood, your lordship."

"Then, perchance, many lives have been needlessly sacrificed?" It was the Doña Isabel who asked the question, and her host's bronzed cheeks flushed darkly as he slowly answered, "Gracious lady, doubtless there have been!" He said no more, either in explanation or extenuation of his deeds, for a flood of disagreeable memories surged over him and choked his utterance. Admiring his frankness, but pitying his evident distress, Lady Isabel hastily added, "And pearls, brave sir—rumor hath it that they have been also found, since we sailed from Spain."

"In sooth have they," replied Balboa. "And I have a necklace of them that, though they have been slightly injured by the Indian mode of piercing them, are good to behold. He then called a servant, who, in obedience to his whispered order, went into another room and soon returned with the pearls.

"By your leave, lady, let me show you these," said Balboa to Doña Isabel, who, at sight of the pearls, exclaimed outright, in pure ecstasy of delight: "Why, they are the most perfect and beautiful in all the world! None like these have I seen, even at the court of my queen."

"But, I trust, some time these may be seen at the court of the king, my lady, and that you may wear them there!"

"Why—how can that be?" asked Doña Isabel, in surprise.

"If his excellency will allow me, and if you, fair lady, will accept from me, these baubles, then are they yours," rejoined Balboa, rising from his seat and bowing, with his hand upon his heart.

"No, no," she exclaimed, hastily, but yet fondling the necklace admiringly, "it cannot be."

"Ay, but it can," said her husband, gruffly, his small, black eyes twinkling with avarice. "As I take it, this gift to thee, Isabel, comes from a portion due the crown, and hence belongs to me as well as to thee—if so be the king himself doth not lay claim to it, forsooth."

"Nay, nay; not so!" exclaimed Balboa, the hot blood rising to his brow, his eyes sparkling with anger. "The king hath had his fifths, justly apportioned before we took our shares, and a donative besides. These pearls are—that is, they were—*my* pearls, and if I chose to bestow them upon the Doña Isabel, your excellency, as her husband, has only the right to refuse them, and that, too, without questioning my motive or my ownership of these pearls."

"Our host, the gallant cavalier, is right," interposed the bishop. "He hath, in a most magnificent manner, done honor to thee, Don Pedro, and to thy wife, by despoiling himself of treasure that must have cost him dear, and presenting it to the Lady Isabel. It ill becomes thee, Pedro, to receive this precious gift so sourly. Verily," he added, with a sigh, "it is a gift worthy of acceptance by the Church!"

"I have reserved for thee and for the Church a tithe of the gold that was apportioned me, good father," declared Balboa.

"And for me what hast thou?" demanded Pedrarias.

"My services, your excellency, which are potential gold and pearls! For the wilderness contains much which has not yet been revealed, and which I have not had time to seek."

"Since that be so, suppose you, to-morrow, give me an account of your stewardship: an exact statement concerning the country and the savages, which I may send to the king."

"It shall be forthcoming, your excellency; but not to-morrow, I fear, since much have I to do, as well as much to write. Within the week will I have it ready for your perusal."

"Be it so, then, and see to it that the report is comprehensive as to the regions of gold and the great South Sea, which, I understand, you claim to have discovered."

"Which, of a truth, I *did* discover," answered Balboa, indignantly, "Many had sought it, as you should know, but none had found it, or the way thereto, until I, Vasco Nuñez de Balboa, showed the way. Mayhap I be deprived of fortune and of life, but of the honor, the immortal glory, of that discovery, none shall rob me!"

"There lives no man who could, perhaps none so base as to desire to," exclaimed Doña Isabel. Her voice trembled, not alone with indignation but with fear; for at her side sat the one man base enough to do such a thing, and that man was her husband. Pedrarias was possessed of a crabbed disposition that made him envy every man who had done something worthy of renown, and hate him who stood in the pathway of his own ambition. Hence he hated Balboa with a bitter, unreasoning hatred, and, as his wife had divined, was already scheming to deprive him of his laurels.

This conversation, at the frugal repast spread by Balboa for his guests, will show the trend of occurrences at and during the first week after the arrival of Pedrarias. He landed at Darien already prejudiced against its original settlers, and especially their leader, whom he was not satisfied to have superseded, but determined to degrade, bring to ruin, and if possible to an ignominious ending. The plot of this story will henceforth contain five principal characters: Pedrarias, Balboa, Bishop Quevedo, Espinosa the lawyer, and Doña Isabel. The governor and Balboa were soon at open enmity, the former persistently seeking to circumvent the latter, assisted by the lawyer, and sometimes opposed by the bishop, but frequently foiled by Doña Isabel, who was at heart the persecuted victim's only friend.

XVI

IN THE DOMAIN OF THE DRAGONS

1515

BALBOA faithfully complied with his promise to render the governor an accurate account of the land's resources, giving him, within a few days' time, a list of the mountains, rivers, and ravines where he had found gold in the virgin state; a statement of the colony as he had governed it; his discovery of the South Sea and the route thither; a description of the pearl islands and their wealth; and, finally, the names of the caciques, more than twenty in number, with whom, through force of arms or diplomacy, he had made treaties of peace.

Having obtained this invaluable information from his rival, Pedrarias threw off the mask of friendship which he had assumed for the purpose, and immediately ordered a judicial investigation into his conduct as the self-elected governor of Darien without sanction of royal authority. This scrutiny was conducted by Espinosa, as the only lawyer in the colony, and as he was completely dominated by Pedrarias, his findings were exactly in accordance with his desires. Very soon the unfortunate Balboa was involved in a legal net from which he could not extricate himself until he had parted with more than ten thousand ounces of gold—the greater part of his fortune. Much of his wealth, however, was absorbed by the wily Quevedo, who, as bishop, exerted his influence in favor of the accused, after having received from him a share in his enterprises, considerable gold, and a drove of Indian slaves.

The scope of the inquiry, too, did not satisfy Pedrarias, for the inexperienced lawyer went too largely into the discoveries and invaluable services of Balboa to the crown, instead of confining himself to his arbitrary acts in expelling Enciso and indirectly causing the death of Nicuesa. The result was that through the remonstrances of the bishop and the intercession of Doña Isabel—"upon whom the discoverer never ceased to lavish costly presents, which he mingled with all the politeness and attentions of the most refined courtier"—the governor was induced to cease his persecutions for a while. It had been his intention to send his rival to Spain, loaded with chains and charged with crimes that would compel his conviction before the highest court; but the bishop represented to him that to do so would be the surest way to advance Balboa's interests instead of defeating his ambitions. The king was already aware of his great discoveries, for the world was ringing with the fame of his achievements, so he could not but be rewarded and received with highest honors.

Pedrarias reluctantly abandoned the prosecution openly, but in secret gathered much information from Balboa's enemies which he later used to his injury, and set afloat reports which destroyed his effectiveness and impaired his popularity. He was, in reality, digging the ground from beneath his own feet, as well as undermining Balboa's reputation, for a condition of affairs had developed which demanded all the energies of both leaders in its correction. It was brought about by the governor's recklessness and inexperience, which, combined, had plunged the colony into dreadful calamities.

In the fleet with Pedrarias a vast amount of provisions had been brought to Darien, which with economy would have lasted many months. At first the colonists revelled in abundance; then it was discovered that one ship-load of supplies had been spoiled by sea-water, and soon after another, which had been deposited in a hut on shore, was destroyed by fire. In a short time, in fact, the colonists found themselves face to face with famine, the ravages of which, combined with the evils of the tropical climate, produced a pestilence. In the course of a month no less than seven hundred persons perished, all of them cavaliers who had come with Pedrarias from Spain. A ship-load of the survivors fled the colony, going to Cuba, and a few broken-hearted adventurers reached their homes in Spain, which they had mortgaged for arms and equipments they never had occasion to use. Those who remained at Darien were soon reduced to the last extremity of hunger and despair. They wandered through the streets of Antigua begging for food, and once-wealthy cavaliers of proudest lineage might have been seen bartering their rich ornaments and vestments for a few mouthfuls of cassava bread. Some, who had never before labored with their hands, hired themselves out as wood-cutters or burden-bearers, merely to sustain existence, while others, in the pangs of starvation, fed on grass and the leaves of trees.

One day, says the historian, "a noble knight rushed into the main street of Antigua crying aloud that he was dying of hunger, and, in sight of the whole population, fell, and rendered up his soul. So many perished daily that it was impossible to give them Christian burial, and carts were used for carrying away the dead, as in times of pestilence."

Pedrarias himself was taken with a fever, and, with his wife, was carried to a salubrious spot among the hills, where he soon recovered. Thence he sent orders for the old soldiers to set out, under his second in command, Juan de Ayora, to visit the caciques with whom Balboa had negotiated treaties when on his journey to the sea. This he did with an eye to the occupation of the territory, in order to represent at court that, while his rival might have discovered certain provinces, with their inhabitants, he was the first to occupy and colonize beyond the region of the coast. But Ayora, though he had with him a greater number of soldiers than Balboa had ever commanded in one body, conducted himself with such a reckless disregard for the rights of the natives—seizing the women and children, and putting many Indians to the torture—that the caciques united against and drove him from their territory; so the expedition ended in disaster.

Balboa, meanwhile, was kept inactive at Antigua, and his adherents—for he still had many favorably disposed towards him, who would gladly have followed wherever he led—were not slow in pointing out to Pedrarias the contrast between the old times and the new. "Before you and your minions came," said they, "Antigua del Darien was tranquil within and without. Under the command and control of Vasco Nuñez, she reigned as queen of the isthmus, and gave laws to twenty Indian nations. Our town was well ordered, more than two hundred huts had been erected, the people were cheerful and happy, amusing themselves on their feast-days by jousting with reeds, the soil was cultivated, and all the caciques so pacific that a single Castilian might cross from sea to sea, fearless of violence or insult; whereas at present many Spaniards are dead, the rest dismayed and broken-spirited, and the Indians in insurrection. All this has been caused by the process against Vasco Nuñez. Had he been allowed to proceed in his discoveries, the truth respecting the promised treasures of Dobaybe would ere this have been revealed; the Indians would still have been peaceful, the soil yielding its abundance, and the Castilians content. Give us again Vasco Nuñez as a leader, for he alone can pacify the Indians; he alone knows the secrets of the land."

The jealous and irritable Pedrarias was greatly incensed by the sneers and reproaches of Balboa's friends. "So they want that rebel and that assassin to lead them against Dobaybe? Inasmuch as there could not be another expedition so likely to be defeated as one against that province, thither shall he go—and may the devil catch him by the way, say I."

This the crafty old governor said to himself, by-the-way, and not to others; nor did he reveal his intentions until after the expedition had departed, when it was found to be badly equipped and lacking in many particulars which the careful Balboa, had he been unhampered, would have supplied. He was rejoiced to be actively employed once more, and especially in the search for that mysterious temple and its golden treasure, which had, so far, eluded the Spaniards; but he was disappointed in having to share the command with Luis Carillo, a friend of the governor and a man of small capacity. His veterans also were outnumbered by the recent arrivals, who were more enthusiastic than prudent, and knew nothing of Indian warfare.

Having ascertained that in his former enterprise in search of Dobaybe he had made a mistake in advancing by land, Balboa resolved to approach it by water, and, embarking his force in canoes, entered a large and unexplored river at the head of the gulf. It ran through a swamp infested with vampires and alligators, and also—according to reports of the Indians—the abode of a monstrous dragon which, with its progeny, had been brought there by a hurricane. From what the Indians told the Spaniards they inferred that these monsters were harpies, for they had the faces of men or women, the claws of vultures or eagles, and huge, leathery wings. They were so monstrous that only the largest trees could support them when they alighted, and so fierce and powerful that whenever they espied a man on the ground they would swoop down like a hawk, and, seizing him in their claws, bear him off to their dens in the mountains. Those who had been there affirmed that these dens were littered with the bones of such unfortunates as had been torn to pieces and devoured by the dragons, who seemed to have established themselves as the self-constituted guardians of the golden temple and its idol.

It is doubtful if Balboa believed this tale of the dragons; but if so he did not let it daunt him, and pushed on through the dismal morass by means of the noisome stream that traversed it. Suddenly, on turning a bend of the river, the Spaniards found themselves face to face with an immense swarm of savages in canoes, who proceeded, with howls and yells, to surround them. At the same time they let fly clouds of darts and arrows, by which many soldiers were killed or wounded, while many more were drowned by the vicious savages plunging into the water and overturning the canoes. The two commanders were wounded: Balboa slightly, and Carillo, who was pierced through the breast by a lance, so badly that he shortly died.

The Indians forced Balboa to retreat to shore, where he beat them back, but was compelled to return to Darien through the inundated forests swarming with noxious reptiles, and without having obtained even a glimpse of Dobaybe. The dangers and horrors of that retreat exceeded anything that the brave soldier had previously experienced; and it was his first defeat! His partisans attributed it to the fact that he had not been given absolute command; but those of Pedrarias taunted him with cowardice and weakness, two qualities which, as those acquainted with his life know full well, were not a part of his nature. But he began to fear his evil star had risen above the horizon, and he was downcast, if not dispirited, while in proportion as he was depressed rose the spirits of the rancorous old governor. He exulted greatly in the misfortunes of Balboa, even at the expense of his soldiers, the loss of life being as nothing, in his eyes, compared with the pleasure he experienced by his enemy's downfall.

His rejoicing, however, was of short duration, for soon after Balboa's return Pedrarias received a letter from King Ferdinand, commanding him to consult with his "faithful servant, Vasco Nuñez de Balboa," on all affairs of importance, for, as he would see by the enclosed credentials, he had constituted him adelantado of the great South Sea, and governor of the provinces of Coyba and Panama. He was, however, to be subordinate in authority to Pedrarias, "who, on his part, was charged so to favor and advance the pretensions and enterprises of that chief as might prove to him the esteem in which the king held his person. The court doubtless intended thus to reconcile the respect due to the character and authority of the governor with the gratitude and rewards earned by Balboa; however, that which seemed so easy at court, was impossible in the Darien, where so many passions were constantly in collision."

Pedrarias, in fact, should never have been appointed to control the territory of Darien, which so manifestly belonged to Balboa as supreme executive; but, having made that appointment—unfit and ill-advised as it was—in order to "save face," the king thought to reward the discoverer, and at the same time placate the usurper with the honors of a captain-generalcy. That they were empty and valueless, Pedrarias knew full well, for the rich regions lay within the boundaries of Balboa's territory, while his own government included only the country contiguous to the gulf, which was devoid of intrinsic riches, unhealthy, and impoverished.

For these reasons the choleric Pedrarias, when he received the royal order, fumed and raved, declaring to this wife that never should that rebel and assassin, Vasco Nuñez, be so highly honored at cost to himself. He would withhold the letter, and if possible keep the intelligence secret; but he found this to be impossible, for Balboa's friends at court communicated to him what had been ordered by the king, and he forthwith demanded his rights. In this demand he was joined by the bishop, who denounced this interference with the evident intention of the king as an outrage upon the rights of his friend, and the rebellious governor was quickly brought to terms.

At a council of officials called by Pedrarias sometime in the latter part of the year 1515, Balboa was invested with his titles and dignities, and thenceforth was always addressed as "Adelantado." But the wily old governor had neatly turned the tables on his rival by bestowing upon him, in fact, the empty honors, and reserving to himself the substantial emoluments of office, since he had forced from him a stipulation that he would not enter upon the actual government of his provinces without his permission!

Even the concession he was compelled to make sufficed to fan the smouldering fires of the governor's jealousies to a flame, and he was more than ever convinced that in the person of Balboa he had a deadly rival and insidious foe, who should be removed from his path at whatever cost. It was at this juncture, while the friends of the discoverer were flocking about him with rejoicings, and he himself was openly exultant, that there arrived in the gulf a vessel consigned to him, freighted with arms and ammunition, and containing seventy adventurers, evidently intended for a secret expedition. It was, in fact, commanded by one of his former comrades, Andres Garabito, who had been sent by him to Cuba, several months before, with orders to raise a force and procure an armament for a projected expedition to the Pacific coast.

It may have been Balboa's intention to proceed over the mountains with this armed band and seize upon the government of which he had been deprived by stratagem; but this is unlikely, as the movement was made before he had received the royal title to it. The mere fact, however, that a mysterious ship was off the coast and holding secret communication with the adelantado, was sufficient to rouse the old governor's passions, and in a transport of fury he ordered him to be seized and imprisoned in a wooden cage.

XVII

A COMPACT WITH THE ENEMY

1516

FORTUNATELY for Balboa, his friend the bishop interposed before the governor carried out his intention, and persuaded him, not only to release the prisoner, but to give him the benefit of an impartial inquiry. The inquiry was entered into, but was conducted by the lawyer Espinosa, and so protracted that, though the accused was acquitted of any evil intentions in importing the men and armament, yet he was harassed to the verge of desperation and completely impoverished. Lawyer Espinosa was enjoying a monopoly of all legal processes, owing to the king's prohibition against others of his class, and had already involved nearly every man in the colony in some sort of entanglement, from which he could extricate himself only by paying to the licentiate a good fat fee.

The good offices of the bishop did not cease with a single effort in behalf of his friend, for he recommended him to Pedrarias as the proper person to conduct an expedition across the mountains, to the sea he had discovered, for the purpose of investigating the islands abounding in pearls. This step, however, the yet jealous Pedrarias refused to take. He intended to have the islands explored, but not by their discoverer, as that would only add to the laurels he already wore, and increase his popularity both at Darien and in Spain.

An expedition was formed, consisting of sixty men, commanded by one Gaspar Morales, a relative of the governor, with the redoubtable Francisco Pizarro as his lieutenant. The man whom the world was to know as the conqueror of Peru had already been to the coast with Balboa, and, knowing the way thither, led the party safely to the shores of the Pacific. Leaving thirty men with a cacique named Tutibara, Pizarro embarked with the others for the pearl islands, where he encountered a fierce resistance from the islanders, whom he overcame, after great slaughter had been inflicted, and compelled to pay him tribute. The cacique of the island brought him a basketful of pearls as a peace-offering, among which were several of great beauty and extraordinary size. These he gladly exchanged for iron hatchets, beads, and hawk-bells, sagely remarking, when the Spaniards smiled at his simplicity, "These things I can turn to useful purpose; but of what value are those baubles to me? The shores of this island and the deep places of the waters around them abound in pearls without number, which my divers can get for me whenever I wish."

Taking the Spaniards to the summit of a high hill, and showing them the distant coast of the mainland, with its towering mountains and bluff promontories, he remarked: "Beyond and beyond, as far as you can see, and much farther, lies a land containing a rich kingdom called Biru [Peru], where gold is as plentiful as stones are with us. That is a country worthy your efforts; that is something which will richly reward you—if you can but conquer it." It is thought that then and there, while listening to the cacique of the pearl islands, Francisco Pizarro formed the resolve to seek out and effect the conquest of that golden empire which he subjugated sixteen years later.

We shall have nothing further to do with this expedition, except to relate its results as they bear upon the fortunes of Balboa. It came near sharing the fate of nearly all those which were sent out while Pedrarias ruled the isthmus, for, on the way back to Darien, Pizarro and Morales were fiercely attacked by several caciques, whom they had outraged by their cruelties, and for seven days pursued through the forests in disastrous retreat. Their command was nearly exterminated, and but a remnant arrived at Darien, after enduring incredible sufferings.

The administration of Pedrarias was replete with disaster from beginning to end, and every enterprise he undertook ended in misfortune and disgrace. A valiant captain, Francisco Becerra, undertook to invade the province of Zenu, where, according to report, gold in unlimited quantities could be drawn from the rivers in nets. He had one hundred and eighty men and three small cannon when he entered the forest and bade farewell to the settlement; but never a man of that gallant command came back, nor were the cannon ever recovered. All were swallowed up in the forest, as though the earth had opened and taken the invaders into a subterranean tomb.

While Balboa was detained inactive at the settlement, these various expeditions under inexperienced commanders overran the country, and effected nothing more than had been already—and better—done by the discredited commander who was being consumed by vexation and despair. All the littoral Indians of Darien had been reduced to subjection by him, and the most that was effected by Pedrarias was a reconquest, which was worse than useless, as it roused the rage of the caciques and provoked retaliation. Among those who, though powerful and warlike, Balboa had overcome and compelled to sue for peace was the mountain cacique Tubanamá. He was blunderingly attacked, by orders of Pedrarias, and not only repulsed the Spaniards from his stronghold, but drove them, bootless, back to Darien, where the survivors arrived breathless and panic-stricken. Stripping the slain Spaniards as they lay in the forest, Tubanamá displayed their bloody shirts on poles as banners, and marched his warriors around the walls, striking terror and dismay to the hearts of all within the settlement. The garrison was beleaguered, foraging-parties assaulted, sorties ambuscaded, and such was the alarm, says the good Bishop Las Casas in his history, that the people feared to be burned within their dwellings.

"They kept a watchful eye upon the mountains, the plains, the waving branches of the trees, for their imaginations were infected by their fears. If they looked towards the land, the long, rustling grass appeared to them to be moving hosts of savages; if they looked towards the sea, they beheld fleets of canoes in the distance. Pedrarias endeavored to hush all rumors that might increase the alarm; at the same time he ordered the smelting-house to be closed, which was never done except in time of war. This was done at the suggestion of the bishop, who caused prayers to be offered and fasts proclaimed in order to avert the impending calamities."

The one man by whom these calamities could have been obviated, Vasco Nuñez de Balboa, was by the governor's orders restrained from action and confined, virtually a prisoner, within the walls of Antigua. While courageous and daring enough in the field, he yet possessed an excessive regard for his sovereign and his representatives, hence his servile submission to the persecutions of Pedrarias. He has remained silent for a long while beneath the governor's opprobrium and calumnies; now let him speak in his own behalf. While the ravage of Tubanamá was in progress, and his warriors were raging around the settlement, he approached the bishop one day as he emerged from the rude chapel that served as church and cathedral. "Your lordship," he said, "I can endure this no longer! My patience, beneath the insults and indignities which the governor has heaped upon me, has reached its limit. Even the king, were he to know all that has occurred in this colony since that base usurper came here, could not but sustain me in rebelling against his authority. He has, as you know, kept me here in durance, while others have been intrusted with expeditions that have invariably returned in disaster. In justice to the survivors of this once-flourishing colony, which I alone placed on a basis of prosperity, but which Pedrarias has reduced to lamentable ruin, I demand that I be established in power again. If not here at Darien, then on the coast of the great sea, of which so little has been learned since I discovered it." His eyes flashed, his breast heaved with deep emotion, and the bishop saw that he was at last aroused from his lethargy—that the lion within him was crouching for a spring.

He heard him through without interruption, then said, soothingly: "My son, it is even so as thou hast said. I have beheld these things with grief and inward rage; but, as thou knowest, Don Pedro hath been appointed by the king, and, though he be technically a usurper, still he is supported by the crown. Had but Arbolancha arrived a few weeks sooner than he did all might have been in thy favor; but now—now the king's eyes have been opened too late to bestow upon thee thy deserts. But patience, my son, for yet a little while. To-day, this very morning, will I see the governor and plead thy cause."

The good bishop quickly redeemed his pledge, and within an hour was in the presence of the governor and his lady. Without a moment's delay he plunged into the subject of which he was so full, representing to Pedrarias that "by keeping the finest capacity in the land in idleness and obscurity he was injuring none more than himself, thus losing the fruits which the friendship of Vasco Nuñez would produce for him."

"There is no doubt," he said to the surly Pedrarias, "that Vasco Nuñez will, in some way or other, make known to the king the oppression and contumely in which he has been held, to the defiance of royal command and the injury of his majesty's interest. Why, then, persist in driving a man to become your deadliest enemy whom you may grapple to your side as your firmest friend?"

"Why, forsooth?" exclaimed Pedrarias, with a growl. "Because he has chosen to oppose me and to oppose the royal commands. But even were we disposed to agree—of which there is doubt—how could I, now that I have humbled and discredited him, still regain his confidence and friendship? It is incredible!"

"Nay, Pedro," said the bishop, bending forward and bestowing a glance full of meaning upon his listeners. "To the contrary, it is the simplest thing in the world. You have two marriageable daughters. Give him one of them!"

"What? One of our daughters marry that base-born caitiff? Hearest thou that, Isabel?"

"I hear," replied his wife, demurely. "But I do not consider Vasco Nuñez so far beneath us that he could not aspire. He is of the hidalguia [nobility] by birth, and not base-born, my lord."

"Aha! the rope of pearls! Hath it, then, bound thee to Balboa?"

"Shame! Thou knowest it is not so. That remark is unworthy of thee, Pedro," exclaimed the bishop, hotly.

Doña Isabel did not respond, but her eyes flashed until their fire was extinguished by the tears that welled up from them. She was used to insult from her lord, but not yet calloused.

Bestowing upon her a glance of sympathy, the bishop continued: "My friends, Vasco Nuñez would be a suitable match for your daughter. He is a man of merit, an hidalgo by birth, and—whether thou likest or not to hear it, Pedro—a favorite of the king. Whilst thou art advanced in years, Pedro, he is in the prime of life, in the very vigor of his days. Make him, then, thy son-in-law, and as thy lieutenant he can carry out thy plans. Thus all his achievements will redound to the advancement of thy family, and to the credit of thy administration."

"Enough!" exclaimed Pedrarias, won over, not so much by the bishop's earnestness and eloquence as by the evident advantages to himself in such a match. "Send for Vasco Nuñez and for a notary. He shall espouse Maria, our eldest daughter. She is in Spain; but that matters not, so the marriage agreement be written out and signed before witnesses. Send for my son-in-law!"

XVIII

BUILDING THE BRIGANTINES

1516

THE life led by Vasco Nuñez de Balboa in the New World, accustomed as he had been to scenes of rapine and to the indulgence of the baser passions, was not conducive to the upbuilding of an elevated character. But that he had a shred of manliness remaining, was shown when, in response to the command of Pedrarias, he presented himself before that worthy at his official residence. When he learned of the compact that had been proposed by the bishop and sanctioned by the governor, he at first seemed stunned by the intelligence; but recovering himself with an effort, he exclaimed: "And this is to be the purchase of my freedom? Bound by pledges which cannot be broken, I am to be delivered into the hands of mine enemy! Never! never will I consent to such a compromise. It is disgraceful, humiliating!"

"Tut, tut," said the bishop. "You forget, my son, in whose presence thou art speaking: the head of thy Church, the head of the government—not only—but before a lady of a rank the equal of, if not exceeding, thine own."

"I crave her pardon," said Balboa, now for the first time allowing his gaze to rest upon Doña Isabel. "But do you, my lady, approve this alliance? As the mother of your daughter, and knowing me for what I am—what I have been in this wild land—do you consent to such a sacrifice?"

"She is my eldest, and dear to my heart," responded the Lady Isabel; "but I not only consent to—I approve of this arrangement."

"Then so be it," rejoined Balboa, with a sigh. "Never have I seen the maiden; but if she be like her gracious mother, then truly shall I be the most fortunate of men." He advanced, and bowing low before her, with courtly dignity, pressed his lips to the hand which she extended.

"Most fortunate of men, indeed," exclaimed Pedrarias, with a sneer; "not only in what you gain, but what escape. Dost hear, Isabel? he *condescends* to marry our daughter! We will make note of that; but, inasmuch as I have decided, we will for the moment overlook it. Now the notary, and the marriage compact. These, our signatures, you witness, notary. Enough. It is done; it is affirmed. Maria shall be sent for, and when she arrives the marriage shall be solemnized. Now, son-in-law, what is it thou desirest most of all—saving, of course, to be my son-in-law?"

"Your excellency," responded Balboa, ignoring the sneering tone and look, "when you came hither it was my intention soon to build some ships, and, after transporting them to the coast of the new sea, to explore its shores and islands."

"Then proceed. It is a good intention, and should be carried out at once. But how, son-in-law, wilt transport the ships across the mountains? The way is long and rugged—impossible."

"Nay, not impossible. After what has been achieved, it is feasible. At the port of Acla, in Careta's country, I would fain cut the timbers, collect the material for fittings, and thence have them taken by carriers to the southern sea-coast."

"Good! In the province of Careta, another father-in-law of thine, by the way, thy relations with whom thou must sever! Thou canst not but understand what I mean?"

"I understand," rejoined Balboa, "and your law is my will."

"Certes, thou shouldst have no other, henceforth, as thou'lt find!"

This allusion to Cacique Careta had reference, of course, to the fact—which was well known in Darien—that his daughter, the Cacica, was still held in regard by Balboa, and had not yet returned to her father. Perhaps Doña Isabel had not been aware of the circumstances, for she looked inquiringly at Balboa, who avoided her gaze, and retired in confusion from her presence.

Then ensued scenes of activity at Antigua del Darien to which it had long been a stranger. When it became known that Pedrarias and Balboa were again in accord, the settlers took heart and began to improve their condition. Establishing himself at Acla, a port in Careta's province, to the west of Antigua, where he had already erected a fortress, Balboa began the construction of four brigantines. Timber for two of them was already hewn and shaped, when it was discovered that, having been cut near the sea-coast, it was subject to the ravages of destructive worms, and all the work had to be done over again.

During long weeks and months, troops of negroes and Indians trudged painfully over the rugged trails of the mountains, from the north coast to the south, bearing heavy loads comprised of rigging, anchors, and iron-work for the brigantines, arms, ammunition, and provisions, a distance of fifty or sixty miles. Timber for the second pair of brigantines was felled on the banks of a river called the Balsa, which flowed into the South Sea; but hardly had it been cut and shaped before a flood came down from the mountains and swept it nearly all away. Then, a third time, did the indefatigable Balboa set his men an example by Herculean labors, and after almost incredible toil, exposure, suffering from famine and sickness, two brigantines were finally constructed and floated on the river. They drifted down to the sea-coast, and there, while timber for the other two was being prepared and their fittings brought from Acla, Balboa equipped them with sails and set forth upon the bosom of the ocean he had discovered three years before. This, he thought, was the consummation of his labors and the triumph of his genius; but before him yet lay the country in which he hoped to round out his career by a grand and startling conquest.

A trial trip was made to the islands of pearls, on one of which, called *Isla Rica*, or the Rich Island, he established a base of supplies, and then, with one hundred men aboard his clumsy brigantines, he set sail for the coast of the mainland, where it stretched away to the west and the southward. He was then, if he had but known it, on the watery highway to Peru, but which another was to traverse, to its ending at the gateway of the golden empire. He had found the way, however, and was content, for, with four brigantines soon to be under his orders, and three hundred men in his command, it seemed to him that the treasures of Peru now lay open before him. He could exploit them at his leisure, he thought, and when a school of whales appeared ahead of his vessel—which he mistook for reefs—and a contrary wind assailed him, he abandoned his cruise to the southward and returned to Isla Rica.

Balboa was a careful commander, and he had been three years dreaming of and preparing for the invasion of Peru. He would not, then, jeopardize his chances by starting out half equipped, with less than one-third the number of men he desired and in all probability needed. So he returned to Isla Rica, which, having reduced its people to subjection and investigated its resources, he planned to make his headquarters.

With what exultation he found himself at last free from the domination of Pedrarias! With what delight he rambled over his island realm and thought upon the freedom that would be his, the glorious opportunities unfolded, the treasure he would obtain, when, at last afloat, with armament complete, he would bear down for the land that then lay dim and shadowy upon the horizon!

But, even while indulging in these dreams of future conquest, sinister rumors reached him from the northern shores of the isthmus. At least, viewed in the light that Pedrarias was now his friend, they seemed so, for they related to the arrival of a new governor, who might not look with favor on his schemes, and indeed supplant him with favorites of his own. After consulting with the most trusty of his officers, he resolved to send a messenger to Acla, in order to ascertain the exact condition of affairs in Antigua, for reports were conflicting, and he knew not what to do. The man selected for this important mission was none other than Andres Garabito, who had brought the contingent of armed men from Cuba. Balboa thought he could trust him, as they had campaigned together, passed through perils together, and existed in close comradeship for years; but he had not taken into the account a recent occurrence which had changed Garabito's friendship into bitter hatred.

His enmity was secret, but was none the less vindictive, and it was occasioned by his fondness for Careta's daughter, of whom Balboa claimed sole proprietorship. When, therefore, he one day discovered Garabito paying her attentions—which she seemed not to receive unwillingly—he rebuked his subordinate severely, and sent him away in anger. The occurrence faded quickly from Balboa's mind, for his generous nature did not harbor resentment long; but not so with Garabito, who felt he had been unjustly treated, and meditated revenge.

Before setting out with Balboa on this very expedition, he wrote to Pedrarias that his prospective son-in-law was so completely enamored of the Indian girl Cacica that, rather than give her up, he would fly with her to the wilds and abandon the settlement forever. This poisoned missive had done its dastardly work most effectually during Balboa's absence on the southern coast, and when, by a sinister coincidence, Garabito was chosen to return to Darien to spy upon the Spaniards there, he found the mind of Pedrarias ripe to receive any accusation whatever against the man he hated yet had so highly honored. He was furious from wounded pride and jealousy. His former suspicions revived, and were augmented by the arrival of the malignant Garabito at Acla. This despicable wretch allowed himself to be arrested as a spy, and when threatened with punishment pretended to reveal what he knew and suspected of Balboa's intentions. He declared that his chief intended, as soon as the brigantines were ready for sea, provisioned and equipped, to embark upon the southern ocean. As an independent commander, said Garabito, he proposed to sever all relations with the government of Darien, and cast off his allegiance to the king. Thus was Balboa accused of the crime of treason by this dastard scoundrel, a crime which, as he well knew, was punishable with death!

As the new governor had died in the very harbor of Antigua before he could take up the burden of government, Pedrarias was not only undisturbed, but at liberty now to proceed unrestrained with his persecution of Balboa. In his blind fury, he cast all considerations of justice or fairness to the winds, and listened to the accusations of Balboa's enemies, who now rose up on all sides to condemn him. The colony was again thrown into a ferment by the several factions, for Balboa still had many friends besides those who were with him on the coast; and every advantage which had been gained by the alliance between the governor and the discoverer was thus thrown away. The interests of the colony were subordinated by Pedrarias to the gratification of his malice, and all enterprises halted while he pursued his enemy to the last extremity.

Garabito had, as though unintentionally, let drop that his chief had sent for Cacica, who was instructed to join him in his camp at Isla Rica, he said, without delay. But this was an untruth, for Balboa had broken with her from the day he had promised Pedrarias to do so. As an honorable man—according to the code of honor at that time—he felt himself constrained to abide by the letter of his marriage agreement with the governor's daughter, and had held himself aloof from all temptations. His deep regard for Doña Isabel constrained him also; for, though she had condoned his past, she expected him to comport himself like a true knight in the future. As the mother of his bride in prospective, and as the first pure woman he had met in many years, he regarded her with worshipful reverence. For her sake he had resolved to crucify his lusts and purge himself of all iniquities.

But Balboa's righteous resolve had been made too late, for the Cacica, though she had long since steeled her heart against her master, was piqued at his coldness, and it was that which had caused her to receive the attentions of Garabito, who failed not to tell her of the marriage contract with the governor's daughter. Balboa had, then, at least two enemies who, with a desire for revenge, though from different motives, aided Pedrarias in fastening the fetters upon him.

If this were but a story of love and revenge, rather than the simple biography of a historical character, we should find the material at hand for a most fascinating romance; and if the reader will recall the leading features of chapters v. and ix., in this connection, perhaps such a story may be woven, after all! For we have all the essentials for a plot: valiant hero, beautiful heroine, despicable villain; love, intrigue, the deadly enmity of a base tyrant; and finally, a tragic ending. This final tragedy we are leading up to now, and we shall attempt to show how Vasco Nuñez de Balboa's crimes in the early part of his career came to be visited upon him when at the height of apparent prosperity and power, and brought him to the headsman's block!

When Pedrarias heard from Garabito that the Cacica had been ordered by Balboa to join him on his expedition, he sent an officer to bring her before him. She came tremblingly, having in mind the tortures to which her brother had been subjected when summoned before a similar council by the magistrates. She was waylaid by Garabito, who whispered in her ear: "You have only to say that your master sent for you, but that you refused to go. If you testify otherwise, you are lost, for the governor will put you to the torture!"

The power of Garabito was in the ascendent, over that of Balboa, and the girl testified as he commanded, greatly to the satisfaction of the governor, who grimly regarded this rival of his daughter with something like approval. Her evidence was the last link in the chain he was forging to connect his enemy with treason towards the king. The fact that he had sent for her proved his intention of making the southern coast his base of operations and place of permanent abode. It also showed, the governor argued, that Balboa had no thought of fulfilling his obligations to his daughter, whom he thus virtually repudiated. This thought enraged him to the verge of frenzy. That he should have meditated an alliance with this base-born adventurer (as he styled him then) was exasperating; but that the graceless fellow should have spurned that alliance, and preferred an Indian female to his high-born daughter, stirred his malignant nature to its depths.

XIX

IMPRISONED AND IN CHAINS

1517

WHILE his enemies were plotting to take his life, Balboa was beyond their reach at Isla Rica, where, all unconscious of the dangers that menaced him, he was completing preparations for the voyage southward to Peru. He had sent for and expected supplies and reinforcements, but while they were, presumably, on the way, he did not abate his diligence for a moment.

He relaxed, however, his strenuous exertions, for the great object of the past months of terrible toils had been in a measure accomplished in the building of the brigantines. While the work went on beneath his eye, he allowed himself a little recreation, and amid the delights of Isla Rica indulged in dreams of future conquests. One evening, while reclining in company with some comrades on a couch of palm-leaves spread upon the sands, he pointed to a particular star in the heavens above them, and said: "There is the planet that holds my fate in its keeping. See you yon star, my friends? Well, I was told by Micer Codro (the Venetian astrologer who was with us, you remember, when we first found these shores) that when that star appeared in this position in the firmament my life would be in jeopardy. But should I survive this period of peril, I would become the richest, the most renowned man in the Indies!

"Now, what think ye, comrades? That was more than three years ago, and, according to Micer Codro's prophecy, I should be in peril of my life; yet here am I, almost within reach of my desires, sound in health, with four brigantines and three hundred good men at my command, and on the point of exploring the great Southern Ocean, which I was the first to find! Out upon all astrologers, say I. That man is surely womanish who gives credit to diviners, and especially to old Micer Codro. Star, I salute thee! Continue thou to shine; but thy baleful radiance is not for Vasco Nuñez de Balboa!"

"He was a learned man," replied one of his companions. "Of a truth, I have heard fearsome stories of his sagacity. But what is that? See, yonder on the sea: a canoe approaches. What can fetch a boat hither from the main, save unwelcome tidings?"

"I cannot conceive," rejoined Balboa, "except that the new governor has arrived and it is a summons for us to return. But we shall see as to that, for while the isthmus intervenes between him and me, no power shall stay us nor cause us to delay."

Propelled by the sinewy arms of naked Indians, the canoe darted over the sea and through the surf to the strand, when a man in the garb of a king's official leaped out and approached the group. Going up to Balboa, who was standing expectantly, he bowed low, then said: "Señor Adelantado, a letter I bring you from his excellency the governor."

"Which I receive as his dutiful servant," answered Balboa, taking it in his hand, and reading it by the light of a torch held by one of his aids. "It seems my intended father-in-law is desirous of seeing me and consulting with respect to our projected expedition," he explained to his comrades. "As his wishes are my desires, I shall start in the morning. Meanwhile I am gone, Francisco Companon, you will be in command of the ships and the soldiers. Messenger, what tidings in Antigua del Darien? For, sooth, my father-in-law says not a word as to happenings there. Is all well? Has the new governor arrived? Perchance not, else Pedrarias would not have written."

"The new governor, who was to supersede his excellency, died as he entered the harbor," answered the messenger; but he was silent, or evasive, as to other happenings at Antigua.

On the shore of the mainland other messengers were in waiting, who, finding that Balboa had set out unarmed and without a suspicion of the fate that was in store for him, consulted together as to the advisability of informing him. They did not do so, however, until the mountains were passed and the little party drew near Acla, when, won by Balboa's frankness and open conduct, their sympathies prevailed over their fears of the governor's vengeance, and they informed him of the snare into which he was hurrying. Balboa was astounded, and at first refused to believe in the perfidy of the man to whose daughter he was pledged in marriage.

"I am innocent of any evil intention," he finally exclaimed. "Faithfully have I served Pedrarias, and faithfully have I served my king. No, I will not retreat," he said, in answer to a suggestion that he should escape while the opportunity offered. "I have done nothing worthy of punishment, and I will go forward, for my innocence I can prove."

"To-morrow it will be too late," answered one of the messengers, "for at Acla awaits Francisco Pizarro, with a command, to arrest you. Adelantado, we entreat you: return while you may."

"Nay, never! My back I have never turned to an enemy yet. But I cannot believe that Pedrarias will continue my enemy; and as for Francisco Pizarro, have I not reared him in the profession of arms? Have we not campaigned together, fought and starved together?"

Sorrowfully, then, the little band of unarmed Spaniards held on their way to Acla, in the environs of which they were met by Pizarro and a company of soldiers, who barred the way. Pizarro drew from his corselet an order of arrest and proceeded to read it, while Balboa regarded him with reproachful astonishment. When it was concluded, he exclaimed: "How is this Francisco? You were not wont to come out in this fashion to receive me!" His former comrade made no reply, for he was only obeying the orders of his superior, and had no alternative but to choose between the two: Pedrarias, supreme in authority, and Balboa, discredited commander. He chose to serve the former, and, as shown in the light of future events, he may have chosen wisely, for it was under Pedrarias, then governor of Panama, that he made his first voyage southward, eventually achieving the conquest of Peru, and tearing Balboa's laurels from his brow.

At a muttered command from Pizarro, two soldiers stepped forward with manacles, which they placed upon Balboa's wrists and ankles, and in chains he was conducted to Acla and thrown into prison. There he was soon visited by the wily Pedrarias, who could scarce conceal his exultation at having in his power the man he hated because his reputation was greater than his own. But, concealing his true feelings, he said to Balboa: "Be thou not afflicted, my son. Thou art here through the charges brought against thee by Alonzo de Puente, who, being the king's treasurer, hath compelled me to this proceeding. But, doubtless, an investigation will not merely establish thy innocency, but serve to render thy zeal and loyalty to the crown the more conspicuous."

Balboa made no reply, for, frank and generous himself, without the power of dissembling, he despised, detested a hypocrite. He knew that Puente's charge was a mere pretence behind which were cloaked deeper designs than had yet been revealed; and so it proved, for when, in the course of a few days, Pedrarias was satisfied that the grounds of the legal process were sufficiently strong to secure Balboa's conviction of treason and enable him to put his unhappy prisoner to death, he threw off the mask. Returning to the prison, he said to Balboa, with the hard and threatening countenance which he habitually wore: "Hitherto I have treated you as a son, because I gave you credit for fidelity to the king, and to me, in his name. Since, however, I find myself mistaken, you have no longer to expect from me the conduct of a father, but of a judge and an enemy, as I shall henceforth treat you."

"As for your feelings towards me," indignantly replied the prisoner, "it matters not to me one whit; but as to my conduct towards the king, my sovereign, your charges are false! If what you impute to me were true, holding as I did at my command four ships and three hundred men, by whom I am beloved, why should I not have gone straight to sea without permitting anything to impede my purpose? Safe in the consciousness of my innocence, I returned at your command; and little did I dream of being treated so rigorously and with such enormous injustice. This is my reward for trusting you: a dungeon, with slander, indignities, and chains."

"Yea, traitor," rejoined Pedrarias, hotly, "a dungeon is truly your merited reward for despising the alliance I would have made with you. Truly, I shudder to think of what my family has escaped: of the foul blot which the marriage of my daughter with one of your stamp would have spread upon my proud escutcheon. And all the time you had an Indian mistress, for whom you sent to accompany you on the expedition which would have placed you well beyond my reach. But know, traitor and scoundrel, that she has confessed, and thus the means by which you would have covered my daughter's name with obloquy have been those for encompassing your own destruction!"

"Who, Cacica, the pledge of amity between me and Careta? She has confessed? Nothing had she to confess, for I sent her no message. After my word was given to you that I would not see her, of a truth, I saw her no more. You are a liar, Pedro Pedrarias, and were I but free, with my good sword in hand, fain would I render you unable to utter more false statements against me and those who were once true to me!"

"Ha! Would you, then? Here, jailer, double this fellow's irons, and if he protest, weight him to the floor with them! My throat you would slit, eh? Old as I am, you will find that when it comes to the cutting of throats, Don Pedrarias de Avila needs not rely upon his own unaided sword. There is one in my employ who wields a more potent weapon—mark you—and that is Gomez, the headsman. I go to tell him now to sharpen his axe for four!"

"For four?" exclaimed Balboa, as the old man retreated from the cell. "Who else have you enmeshed in your net, base wretch? Will not one victim suffice you? Who are they? Tell me."

"Who?" repeated the old man, mockingly, peering at his victim through the bars. "Why, who but Hernan de Arguello, Hernan Muños, Valderrabano, and Botello. Were they simply your friends, it were enough; but they are more: they are traitors to the king, and to me, Pedrarias de Avila, governor-in-chief of Darien, whose authority you have endeavored to usurp."

"They, my officers, condemned to die merely because they were friends, and loyal to me," groaned Balboa as, left in the solitude of his cell, he sank helpless to the floor. "Truly is this Pedrarias a fiend, an intimate of the devil, and scarce human! And they will die, being my friends, but no man's enemies."

Realizing that he had proceeded so far it was impossible to leave Balboa alive in the same land with himself, Pedrarias left no stone unturned to accomplish his death. Urged to activity by promise of the command of Balboa's expedition in the event of his death, the vile lawyer, Espinosa, found an indictment against the five which warranted his master in proclaiming they were doomed to die for treason against the king. The proclamation was made at Acla, and not in Antigua, where resided most of the settlers, because, as Pedrarias knew, it would provoke an uprising of the people.

While they were supremely loyal to the crown, and, in their timidity, afraid to declare against its representative, Pedrarias, the people of Darien were yet well inclined towards Vasco Nuñez de Balboa, and most of them his friends, because of his possessing many lovable qualities which the governor lacked.

When, affrighted at the vindictiveness of Pedrarias, Espinosa explained to him that the verdict against Balboa was technical only, and that on account of his great services he should be inclined to mercy, the fiend replied: "No, if he has merited death, let him suffer it. Die he must, and shall, and on your head be his blood!"

XX

THE END OF VASCO NUÑEZ DE BALBOA

1517

WE are compelled, in this chapter, to narrate the details of a horrible crime, to commit which the name of justice was invoked by its perpetrator, Pedro Arias de Avila, the one-time governor of Darien. We have followed the hero of this story, Vasco Nuñez de Balboa, through the various stages of his career: a penniless adventurer, self-elected governor of Darien, savior of the settlement when on the point of dissolution, subjugator of the caciques, discoverer of the Pacific, faithful servant of the king, builder of the first brigantines that ploughed the waters of the great Southern Ocean. We are now to behold him led forth from his prison cell as a criminal, a traitor to his sovereign, and executed in the very town which was founded, through his unwearied efforts, in chief Careta's province.

He was then scarcely forty-two years of age, in the prime of life, seven long years of which had been passed in the wilderness of Darien. He had labored, he had fought, he had committed crimes against humanity—all that his sovereign might acquire a realm beyond the sea—and this was his reward: to perish as a felon, to die as a traitor, "in the full career of his glory, one of the most deserving of the Spanish discoverers—a victim to the basest and most perfidious envy." He had, indeed, deserved well of his king, for of all the Spaniards who explored the regions of America, he was one of the greatest, the most persistent in carrying the flag of his country into unknown lands, in compelling the inhabitants to accept his religion and acknowledge the sovereignty of Spain.

He was not the first of the Spanish explorers and conquistadores to experience that king's ingratitude, nor the last to meet a violent death. Columbus and Cortés died in their beds, but they were victims of their sovereign's neglect. De Soto, worn out by his toils, perished on the bank of the Mississippi, which became his grave. Ponce de Leon, returning to Florida, the land he had discovered, received his death-wound from an Indian arrow. Pizarro was assassinated, by men he had reduced to poverty and exasperated by his taunts.

The reward, then, of exploration and discovery mainly inheres in the accomplishment itself, for few of the world's great explorers have lived to receive the fruits of their labors, as witness Magellan and Hudson and Cook. Of them all, however, perhaps there was none who was so basely requited as

Vasco Nuñez de Balboa. Were it not for the fact that there was in Darien, at the time Pedrarias wreaked his vengeance upon Balboa, a veracious chronicler of events, whose name has survived as author of a great history, we should be loath to accept as true this story of revenge, ingratitude, and crime. But we have it from Gonzalo Fernandez de Oviedo, a contemporary of the chief characters in this tragedy, who was sent out by King Ferdinand as inspector of mines, and who subsequently, as historiographer of the Indies, wrote a great work, which first appeared in 1526. He was intimate with both Pedrarias and Balboa, and after the death of the latter had access to his private papers, from the perusal of which, and from his knowledge of our hero, he drew conclusions as to his merits, which were long since sanctioned by the voice of posterity.

The day arrived in which the sentence of death was to be carried out, and found the little town of Acla overspread with gloom. The horrified inhabitants moved about as in a dream, unable to wholly comprehend the nature of their dread surroundings, hardly daring to allow their tears to flow, much less their voices to be raised in protest. For they realized that in Pedrarias, the governor, they had a man to deal with not in his right mind, warped by envy, malice, jealousy, until he had become a frenzied maniac. They dared not provoke his wrath by protest, even in a whisper, for they were cowards all, rendered so by their subserviency to the crown, which might commit any atrocity and yet be accounted blameless.

Pedrarias had sentenced his prisoner to death in the name of the king, yet he allowed him no appeal, either to the king or to the Council of the Indies; for he knew that sentence would be reversed and the discoverer set free should his voice reach the throne. It never reached it, save as wafted across the sea and ocean in the indignant outcry of the people—after the deed was done by which Balboa lost his head. Then it did not avail to redress Balboa's wrongs nor to bring Pedrarias to justice, for he continued in his crimes for years, and at the last died in his bed, like many another wretch of lesser note.

But the day had arrived, Balboa's last on earth. The hot afternoon wore away, and the sun sank towards the mountains which the prisoner had been the first to explore, and touched with its rays the roofs of the dwellings he himself had erected. The dungeon door was thrown open, and forth came Balboa, preceded by his jailer and loaded with clanking chains. But the burden of the chains was as naught to the armor he had carried in the days of his great deeds, and he bore himself erect, dauntless in mien as of yore.

He searched the village square with flashing eye, sweeping his glance over the assembled crowd of cowards, held back by mailed soldiers under the command of his former comrade and lieutenant, Francisco Pizarro. He was no coward—that Balboa knew; but he had his own reasons for serving

Pedrarias, as already narrated. If Pizarro had but weakened, if he had allowed his sense of justice to prevail over his lust for power and lucre, and said one word for Balboa, all the men under him would have joined in an effort to save the man they loved from him they loathed and hated. But Pizarro was a clump, a stick, a stone—anything inanimate, or, in other words, a soldier—and when Balboa's piercing glance fell on him he looked to the ground and remained immovable.

Preceding the prisoner walked the public crier, who announced: "This is the punishment inflicted by command of the king and his lieutenant, Don Pedrarias de Avila, governor of this colony, upon this man, as a traitor, and usurper of lands belonging to the crown."

"Nay, nay," exclaimed the still loyal Balboa when he heard this lie proclaimed; "it is false! You, my former comrades, know it is false. Never hath thought of such a crime entered my mind. I have ever served my king with truth and loyalty, and ever sought to augment his dominions!"

EXECUTION OF BALBOA

He raised his eyes to heaven and stretched forth his manacled hands, while a murmur of compassion went around the throng in the square of Acla. But there was no demonstration in his favor, for there was no man left in Darien, apparently, with a heart in his breast. The best of Balboa's followers, the original conquerors of the territory, were awaiting his return to Isla Rica, where lay the brigantines ready for exploration, where were gathered the men for a voyage Balboa was never to make, for a conquest he was never to achieve.

There was no man present capable of leading an uprising against the tyrant, save Pizarro, and he was unready. There was no man in authority who could resist the tyrant's authority, for Bishop Quevedo had returned to Spain; but a priest was present, who offered Balboa the sacrament as he ascended the scaffold, and whispered words of consolation. It is doubtful if Balboa heeded them, for, coming from such a source, from a man in the hire of Pedrarias, his words must have seemed meaningless and a mockery.

The rude scaffold stood in the centre of the square, a platform erected on posts, reached by a ladder, which, manacled as he was, Balboa climbed with difficulty. Why he should have climbed at all, and why he so tamely submitted to his fate, seems strange to those acquainted with his courageous nature. But probably the spell of authority was on him, for the magician who had enthralled him had invoked the name of a monster, living afar, but held to be omnipotent. That monster was the king, at mention of whose dread name the most valiant of fighters became servile and abject.

So Vasco Nuñez de Balboa, mistakenly supposing himself bound by the will of a dastard king, went meekly to the scaffold. With a firm step he ascended to the platform, without a tremor viewed the block on which he was to lose his head, and looked calmly on while the grim headsman made it ready. "Now haste," growled the man with the axe, "for there are others, and the sun is low in the sky." Then Balboa gave a start—remembering the others. But it was too late now to save them, and, with a pang at his heart for those he had involved in deadly perils, he sank to the platform and laid his neck on the block. The headsman raised his axe—a thrill of horror ran through the spectators; it fell, and, as the blood spurted from the headless trunk, their groans and lamentations rent the air.

The executioner's work was not finished with Balboa, whose head was held aloft, and then, by orders of the implacable Pedrarias, stuck on a pole, where all might view the gory trophy. The three officers followed, and the head of each was taken off at a stroke. The dusk of evening gathered as the last one was beheaded. But there yet remained another victim, one Arguello, whose sole offence lay in the writing of a letter to Balboa warning him of what Pedrarias intended. The people assembled about the scaffold had witnessed—with what feelings of grief and horror may be imagined!—the execution of four gallant soldiers whose offences were such Pedrarias would not pardon them. But now, overcome by their sympathies, they entreated, with sighs and with tears, that this life might be spared, "inasmuch as God had not given daylight for the execution of his sentence." The stony-hearted governor, resentful and relentless, replied: "Never! Rather would I die myself than permit one of those traitors to escape unpunished!"

Chilled with horror, the people returned to the square, where the scaffold was but dimly visible in the gloom of approaching night, and where the last act of the horrible drama was being performed in darkness. They heard the clank of Arguello's chains as he fell across the block, and then, after an interval of breathless silence, the thud of the axe, proclaiming all was over.

Pedrarias had witnessed all, hidden behind a palisade of reeds, through the crevices of which he watched the doings on the scaffold, less than twenty feet away. There he crouched, a demon in human semblance, gloating over the anguish of the people, the groans of his victims, and counting the strokes of the headsman's axe.

Beneath a tree on the verge of the forest cowered a fearsome watcher, the Cacica, formerly beloved of Balboa. Peering through the screen of leaves, she witnessed the dreadful ending of him whom she had both loved and hated. But she did not exult, like the man-fiend Pedrarias. Believing that her testimony had sealed Balboa's fate, by the reproaches of conscience she was driven into the forest, where (as nothing more was ever heard of her) she probably perished, an outcast from her tribe, and forgotten by her family.

In Antigua del Darien, a broken-hearted woman mourned the gallant Vasco Nuñez de Balboa; for he had been betrothed to her daughter, who, through her father's vengeful deed, was widowed ere she had been made a bride.

FOOTNOTES:

[1] This was the hurricane predicted by Columbus, as narrated in his *Life* by the author of this biography, and it occurred in 1502. For the further adventures of La Cosa, see the *Life of Amerigo Vespucci*, in this series.

[2] Calaboose, from Spanish *Calabózo*, a dungeon or prison.

[3] Don Manuel Josef Quintana, *Vidas de Españoles Célebres*.

[4] By a curious *lapsus* in Keat's otherwise perfect poem, *On First Looking into Chapman's Homer*, Cortés, conqueror of Mexico, is substituted for Balboa, discoverer of the Pacific—

"Then felt I like some watcher of the skies,

When a new planet swims into his ken,

Or like stout Cortez when with eagle eyes

He star'd at the Pacific—and all his men

Look'd at each other with a wild surmise—

Silent, upon a peak in Darien."

Cortés was never at Darien, nor nearer to it than Honduras, or Santo Domingo.